Cape Town to Kruger

Backpacker Adventures in South Africa and Swaziland

JOHN DWYER

DEDICATION

Dedicated to my sweet daughter Hannah, with all
my love and kisses.

CONTENTS

ACKNOWLEDGMENTS

I'd like to thank the following people for their help in making this book possible. A huge word of gratitude goes out to my core editing team of Allen Ambrosino, Steve Warner and Sarah Lovell. This book owes much to their honest feedback and valuable suggestions.

Sincere thanks also to the following for their editing help: Kieran Harrington, Johhny Gilligan, Eoin Canny, Gerard Harrington, Steve Meehan, Dominic Taylor, Noel Phylan, Paul Whiting, Shane McElwee, Louise Zaal and Anne-Marie McKenna.

Very special thanks to my darling wife Caroline, who not only gave me the space and time to write but also helped edit my manuscript.

Any errors in this book are entirely my own.

1 CAPE TOWN

"Please return to your seat, we're about to land," the flight attendant warned me as I gazed out the aircraft window. I had no intention of obeying her, as I drank in my first sight of Table Mountain. Along with a few other giddy passengers, I had ignored the fasten seatbelt signs and rushed to some empty seats on the opposite side of the aircraft to enjoy its majestic presence. Flushed with the golden light of the morning sun, the mountain seemed to be one with the azure sky above. Its ancient cliffs rose dramatically from the city below, abruptly ending with the signature flat plateau that lends the mountain its name. It held me spellbound until the flight attendant returned and sternly ordered me to return to my seat at once. I happily obliged but Table Mountain would continue to captivate me for the remainder of my time in Cape Town.

Situated at the foot of Table Mountain, the lovely Ashanti Hostel would be my home while in Cape Town. The cheery receptionist showed me to a six-person dorm, where the pungent smell of feet hit me as soon as I opened the door. I pretended not to notice and selected a vacant lower bunk. A sockless fellow traveller – I'm not accusing anybody, you understand – lay on the top bunk opposite and I gave him a cheery hello, receiving only a solitary grunt in reply. It felt strange to share a room with total strangers, trusting that none of them suffered from chronic snoring, severe body odour or bed-wetting tendencies. At any rate, I would get very used to dorm life over the next twelve months of world travel.

I unpacked my things before laying on my bunk for a rest. I noticed the base of the bunk above me was lavishly decorated with crude drawings of women's breasts, alongside a roll of honour highlighting the previous occupants. Jacko, Butch, Snake and Wozzer all felt the need to immortalise themselves. I shook my head in disapproval at such needless vandalism before finding a pen and adding my own signature next to a set of boobs that would have made Dolly Parton proud. That little job finished, I lay back and exhaled deeply. My journey had finally begun. All the planning, saving and research was behind me and my adventure of a lifetime had started. It was time to celebrate with my first African beer.

2

At the hostel bar, I asked for a local beer and received a cold Castle lager. I brought it out to the veranda and tried to get through some of Nelson Mandela's book, *Long Walk to Freedom*, but the view kept tearing me away. If there's another city in the world with a better setting than Cape Town, do let me know.

The city is cradled in an awe-inspiring, natural amphitheatre. The giant wall of Table Mountain, flanked by the sentinel peaks of Lion's Head and Devil's Peak, form a protective barrier around the city, while the boat-filled waters of Table Bay lap its distant shore. It was a backdrop that repeatedly succeeded in taking my attention from Mandela's weighty tome.

Long Walk to Freedom is big, both in content and actual size. A backpacker has to justify every ounce of gear they carry, but this 800-page volume was an exception to the rule. Mandela is inexorably linked with South Africa and I felt reading his story would help me better understand his country. Getting through his book over the following number of weeks would be my own *long read to freedom*.

Hunger forced me to finally abandon Mandela and go in search of food. The receptionist recommended a local Italian restaurant a short way from the hostel. I found it easily and took a seat while browsing the menu. A good-looking waitress took my order and I felt it was time to try some Irish charm.

"What do you recommend?" I asked, looking up at her with the brightest smile I could muster. "This is my first day in South Africa," I confessed. On hearing this, she seemed to brighten.

"I hope you'll enjoy my country," she replied. I introduced myself to Antoinette and asked her what to see during my stay in Cape Town.

"Why don't you take my number," she said, scribbling her digits on the back on a white napkin. "Me and my friends would be happy to show you around a bit." A smile as broad as Table Bay lit up my face.

"By the way Antoinette, are you Afrikaner?" I asked.

"Yes," she replied, "and proud to be."

I was curious about the Afrikaners. They were descendants of Dutch and German settlers from the 17th and 18th centuries who spoke a dialect of Dutch called Afrikaans. Universally reviled as the architects of the apartheid system, I wondered how they were adjusting to life under a black government.

Back at the hostel, I celebrated my first night in South Africa by drinking more beer than was good for me. Crawling into my bunk at three that morning, I made a fearsome racket. Mr. Smelly Feet had more than a solitary grunt for me this time, but

I was too drunk and happy to care.

My celebratory mood continued over the next few days as I indulged in a good party, or *jol*, as they say in South Africa. The exchange rate between the local currency, the rand, and the euro was ten to one, with good-quality Castle beer costing fifteen rand. You do the math. I frequented backpacker bars, nightclubs and anything else the city had to offer. My spirits were high and with good reason, as my trip had come close to not happening at all.

My dream of travelling the world with my best friend Eamonn was a year in the planning. We spent hours poring over world maps in the kitchen of the Dublin house we shared. Over copious cups of tea, we agreed on itineraries, disagreed and then agreed again. We proposed and discarded routes like generals plotting troop movements during a military campaign. Red ink circled famous cities such as Cape Town, Perth, Sydney, Auckland, Hong Kong, Hanoi, Bangkok and Delhi. I loved every minute of it.

We finally agreed on a route through South Africa, Australia, New Zealand, China, South East Asia and India. All that was left to do was to purchase the plane tickets. However, disaster struck when Eamonn received a job offer at a company he always wanted to work for. He felt he couldn't commit to the trip at that time and suggested we instead postpone the date of departure by a few months.

I sympathised with his situation but, for me, it was the chance of a lifetime. If I delayed, my dream of world travel might be over. Many times I made up my mind to leave as originally planned, only to reverse my decision the following day. I was confused and didn't know what to do.

The final decision was made after watching the film, *Dead Poet's Society*. Once I understood the film's message of *Carpe Diem*, or *Seize the Day*, I knew what I had to do. I resolved to leave as planned and, if my friend were able, he could join me at a later stage. My decision filled me with relief and joy. I knew this journey was going to be life-changing.

Once my initial merriment in Cape Town abated, along with my hangovers, I got down to the business of exploring the city. I rang Antoinette and arranged to meet her near the city centre.

As I waited for my taxi outside the hostel, I noticed Table Mountain was shrouded in a white blanket of fog, aptly referred to by the locals as the *Tablecloth*. The story goes that a pirate named Van Hunks retired from his wicked life at sea to live on the slopes of Devil's Peak. He spent his days sitting on the mountain, smoking his pipe. One day, a stranger approached and challenged him to a smoking contest. The battle lasted for days, causing smoke to build up and drift towards the town.

When Van Hunks finally won the challenge, the stranger revealed himself as the Devil, hence Devil's Peak, and they both disappeared in a puff of smoke. Whenever Table Mountain is adorned with its tablecloth, locals say that Van Hunks and the Devil are in the midst of another smoking duel.

The taxi took me from the hostel to our meeting point a few miles away. Walking along the city streets, I became hyper-aware of my surroundings. I imagined everyone was staring at me, weighing up a chance to grab my bag or just shoot me in cold blood because I was white.

Coming to South Africa, you cannot help but be aware of its reputation for violent crime. It's almost compulsory to include some shocking statistics when writing about the country, so here it goes. In 2013, there were over sixteen thousand murders, nearly fifteen thousand attempted murders, sixty-six thousand sexual offenses, eighteen thousand homes robbed by armed gangs, and nearly ten thousand vehicle hijacks. To put this into context, the murder rate is six times higher than the United States and thirty-one times higher than the United Kingdom.

Even the police themselves contribute to these horrific statistics. In 2011, the head of the Crime Intelligence Division was investigated for serious offenses, including murder and corruption. At the time of writing, the investigation was still ongoing.

Be in no doubt, South Africa is a violent country.

After meeting Antoinette and her friends, Tani and Harko, we set off towards the Cape of Good Hope in their car. All three were young and full of life. Their car was adorned with bumper stickers that read 'Smoke Weed' and 'I Love Africa'. Harko drove with the window down, letting the rushing air blow through his mop of black curls. He wore a pair of flip-flops, along with a ripped t-shirt. Antoinette and Tani sat in the back, frequently leaning forward to change the radio station until they found a song they liked.

Once we parked at the Cape of Good Hope Nature Reserve, we made our way towards the shore. Shortly after, a gang of baboons crossed our path. This was my first encounter with these creatures, although I had already read signs near the car park warning people not to feed them.

"Watch out for those bastards," Harko advised me. "Last week, some of them entered a car with the windows open and destroyed the interior. When the owner tried to scare them off, they bared their teeth at him. You don't want to get bitten by a baboon."

Indeed, a baboon's mouth is like a dog's and they have long, incisor teeth. Dependant on food from well-meaning visitors, baboons can become aggressive if not fed regularly.

Surrounded by impressive cliffs, Cape Point

offered excellent views of the immense expanse where the Atlantic and Indian Oceans collide. I shielded my eyes from the sun while watching a distant tanker plough slowly along the horizon. A fresh breeze whipped at my clothing, as seagulls screamed overhead. The four of us walked out as far as we could on a rocky ridge jutting into the sea. There, Antoinette and Tani danced and pirouetted together like a pair of schoolgirls. I looked out at the vast waters, knowing the next landmass beyond those churning seas was ice-bound Antarctica.

"Cape Point," I shouted, lifting my arms into the air in triumph, "the most southerly point in Africa. Did you know this was originally called Cape of Storms by the Portuguese explorer, Bartholomew Diaz?" I said, repeating some newly-acquired knowledge from my guidebook. "It was renamed Cape of Good Hope by the king of Portugal, as it offered good hope for a route to India."

Hands on my hips, I took a deep breath and filled my lungs with Good Hope air.

"I've always wanted to come here and now my dream has come true. Thanks for bringing me out here," I continued, turning to the three. The girls giggled nervously and started gazing at their shoes, while Harko cleared his throat.

"Actually, the most southerly point in Africa is called Cape Agulhas," Harko gently informed me, concern etched on his face. I took this new information on board for a few moments in silence, nobody saying a word.

"So, how far is Cape Agulhas?" I asked Harko, fearing the worst. I clung to the notion we might be able to drive there before dark.

"I'd say about a hundred miles southeast of here, is that about right?" he replied, turning to the girls for confirmation. They both nodded in agreement. I stood there for another minute before Harko came over and put an arm around my shoulder.

"I won't tell anyone if you won't," he said with a broad smile. The girls burst into laughter and I couldn't help but join them.

"Come on, let's go for a beer," I suggested, as we made our way back towards the car park.

On the way, I decided to get their thoughts on life in the new South Africa.

"What do you think of the new government," I asked tentatively.

"Not good for young whites like us, that's for sure," Harko replied, "Corrupt bastards as well."

The girls nodded in agreement, something they seemed to do a lot when Harko was in full flow. "It's hard to get a job as young blacks are now being preferred over whites," he continued, getting pretty agitated at the thought. "It's racism by a different name – positive discrimination," he finished, spitting out the last two words.

"Discrimination is discrimination," muttered Antoinette. "There's no future for us here in South Africa. We'll probably have to leave for London or Australia."

We went back to Ashanti where we spent the evening drinking beer and telling people how I had – almost – stood on the most southerly tip of Africa.

2 TOWNSHIPS AND THE TABLE

I first became aware of South African townships through television coverage of the anti-apartheid riots in 1989. My grandmother had been given a new colour television and I was more than happy to keep her company while watching football matches. She always asked me to switch on the six o'clock news for her, as she found the new remote control difficult to operate.

The main news stories that day were another British soldier killed in Northern Ireland and the escalating violence in South Africa. The report showed black township youths running in all directions as a body lay on the ground, engulfed in flames. The reporter said people who had collaborated with the apartheid government were being 'necklaced' with burning car tyres. I was transfixed in horror at the scene until my father came in and saw what I was watching. He wordlessly switched off the set, telling me to do my homework.

Those awful scenes stayed with me for a long time, but also made me want to visit the townships. After a quick chat with the Ashanti front desk, I was booked on a township tour. The tour bus collected four others and myself from the hostel the following morning. Our guide and driver introduced himself as Brian Smith and told us he was a coloured South African. I have to admit, I wasn't aware of this separate racial group as I always thought coloured was just another term for black. Brian put me straight on this.

"Coloured people are a mix of the native Koi, Malay slaves and early European settlers," he said. "They enjoyed some privileges under apartheid and mostly voted for the ruling National Party."

Our first stop was District Six. Before 1966, the area was a genuine Cape Town melting pot, populated mainly by coloured people, along with Indians, blacks and whites. That was until it was declared a whites-only area in 1966, forcing thousands to flee before bulldozers demolished their homes. The government justified these forced removals by claiming the area was a slum and a hotbed of crime. In reality, its close proximity to the city centre and Table Mountain made it prime real estate. By 1982, the authorities had forced more than sixty thousand people to relocate to the barren Cape Flats area north of the city.

"My family lived here in District Six before we were forced to leave and our house destroyed," Brian told us. He drove along a barren area littered with broken beer bottles and pointed to the left. "Our house used to stand there," he told us, pointing to a patch of ground beside the road. "I remember playing with other kids along this street. It was a busy place, a fun place," he recalled. Now, there was nothing but the faint outlines of former homes to testify it had once been a lively neighbourhood.

The District Six Museum is a memorial to those lost neighbourhoods. Street signs decorated the walls, recalling places that once buzzed with life, such as Russell Street, De Villiers Street and Stuckfris Street. The museum also included wooden benches that bore signs in English and Afrikaans stating, "Europeans only. Slegs Blankes." The tragedy is that after all the homes in District Six were destroyed, international pressure forced a halt to new construction and the area remained a desolate wasteland.

The tour continued to the small township of Langa, meaning 'sun' in Xhosa. It consisted of simple shacks made from sheets of corrugated iron or planks of wood. Many were brightly painted in aqua blue or deep green tones, giving the place a great splash of colour.

"The people are proud of their simple homes and want to keep them clean," Brian told us as we walked around. As if to prove his point, a woman swept the earthen ground as we passed by.

We soon reached a local primary school, housed inside a shed made from corrugated sheets of metal. Inside, the children were in a boisterous mood, as is the way with young school kids the world over. I took some photos while the children waved and pulled faces for the camera. Their colourful drawings dotted the metal walls and brightened the otherwise drab interior. Brian explained the school relied entirely on volunteers and donations to keep it going.

Children at a school in the Langa Township

Once the teacher managed to restore order, the children stood up and sang the national anthem,

Nkosi Sikelel' iAfrika, or *God Bless Africa.* In the West, the importance of education may be taken for granted but not here, that's for sure.

Outside, I joined some kids in a game of soccer on the dusty street. They played with a badly worn tennis ball and I felt like an elephant dancing around a mouse, trying to control and pass the tiny ball. The kids were incredibly skilful, kicking the ball onto their shoulders and knees with ease. They took pity on my awkwardness by kindly complimenting my dubious skills before I departed.

Back in the minibus, we passed through a coloured township. It didn't have much in common with the one I had just seen. Solid redbrick houses lined the litter-free streets, some with gardens of colourful flowers and well-tended lawns. I asked Brian why this was.

"As I said, coloured people got preferential treatment during apartheid," he said. "They were allowed to build brick homes and have access to piped water and electricity. This was only a ploy to separate the non-whites and drive a wedge between them."

"Divide and conquer," I muttered.

"Exactly," Brian replied. "We saw the real apartheid government in action in District Six."

We drove back onto the motorway and, a little later, we got our first view of the Khayelitsha

Township. A Xhosa word meaning 'new home', Khayelitsha was a sea of flat, tin roofs, crushed tightly together with barely a space between them. An electric pylon protruded from this sea, festooned by lines of washing fluttering in the breeze.

"The government says there are 500,000 people living in Khayelitsha, but I assure you the number is closer to two million," Brian said. "This area is called the Cape Flats, poor land to the east of Table Mountain where the apartheid government relocated people from other areas such as District Six."

We meandered through the township, observing everyday life. People bartered at stalls selling an array of unidentified meat products. Other vendors displayed a range of brightly coloured fruit, presided over by big women in flamboyant headgear. Nearby, a sheep's head roasted on a grill, eyes protruding from the blackened skull in a hideous manner. A woman stood alongside, fanning the hot coals with a piece of cardboard. Brian explained these local favourites were known as 'smileys', so called because the scorched sheep head seems to be smiling. Sheep and goats, not yet turned into smileys, foraged for scraps nearby.

"Those women are waiting for cow intestines," Brian said, pointing to the group standing around a bare table. Nearby, a boy held a peeing dog up to a frightened child. Shoe repairmen wandered along the street, carrying their polish-smeared, wooden boxes. A converted shipping container operated as the local barbershop, 'Barber and Phone Repairs' daubed in bright letters on its side. The owner watched from a roughly-cut window on the side of the container, awaiting his next customer. Children gyrated with boundless joy to the rhythm of *Kwaito*, the local reggae music. Despite the poverty, there was great energy and life in Khayelitsha.

The township was a place where nothing was wasted. Corrugated iron sheets, plasterboard, cardboard boxes and tyre rubber were used as building materials. Despite the lack of facilities, people made a great effort to keep the place clean. Electricity is beyond the means of most township homes, even though power lines hung tantalisingly above their shacks. Instead, most people illegally hook wires to the nearest supply.

As we drove around, I caught the eye of a boy sitting on a wooden crate, surrounded by dismembered engine parts. For a brief second, we looked directly at one another. He held my gaze and I raised my hand in a meek salute before he disappeared from view. Suddenly, it didn't feel right, looking at all that squalor and not doing anything to help.

Was I taking part in poverty tourism or was I seeing the real lives of millions of South Africans and getting a more rounded view of the country? What could I do when faced with such want? What should I do? Shower them with money? Make lavish promises of donations when I got home?

Any such gesture would only have been for my benefit, to soothe my feelings of shame because that is what I felt, shame. Once the tour ended, I would return to my hostel, the poor would stay in the township and there wasn't a dammed thing I, or anyone else, could do.

I felt that way until Brian took us to see Rosie's Kitchen, a place that provided food to the needy of the area. Wearing a white apron, Rosie welcomed us to Khayelitsha. She invited us to look inside her home, which was a converted shipping container. From the outside, it didn't look like much. However, she enjoyed modern conveniences such as a satellite television, a microwave and a DVD player. Surrounded by bright, floral wallpaper, her couch was still covered by the protective plastic sheeting.

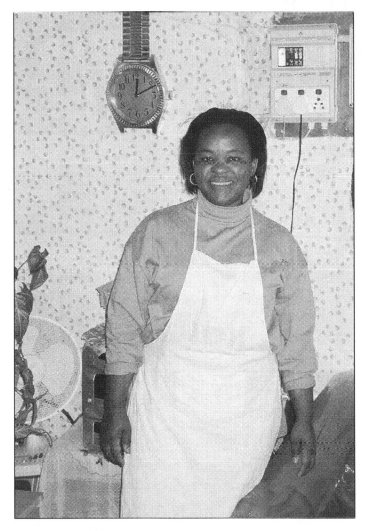

Rosie at her home in Khayelitsha

"Our small kitchen serves 350 people a day, mainly children," Rosie explained as we left her home and walked towards the kitchen outside. "Sometimes, we are short and must turn the adults away but we always try to feed the little ones."

From the open doorway, Rosie pointed into the tiny, wooden kitchen, measuring ten feet by ten. It was hard to imagine how so many meals were prepared in such a small space.

"Rosie is an incredible woman," Brian told me, as we walked around the yard. "She came here from the Eastern Cape with her two young children, looking for her boyfriend who gave her a false address. She had nowhere to stay so some people took pity on her and brought her to live in Khayelitsha. She worked hard to support her children. During the rioting of 1989, Catholic nuns were too afraid to come here with weekly deliveries so Rosie did it instead. That was how her first kitchen started. The nuns never thought this young girl could handle the work on her own but she proved them wrong." Brian glanced at his watch and smiled. "Time for a beer," he said.

Brian led us into a nearby *shebeen*, originally an Irish word for an unlicensed pub. The term is now applied to licensed and unlicensed township taverns across South Africa. During the apartheid era, blacks were barred from entering 'whites-only' drinking establishments and, as a result, illegal shebeens sprang up in the townships. They were an important place for socialising and discussing politics. Today, most of these shebeens are legal.

Once I had a cold beer in my hand, legal or not, Brian continued his story about Rosie.

"Everything was going well for Rosie, as she was working and had her own shack. However, her old boyfriend heard of her success and reappeared. They lived together for a few years before she had an accident and ended up in the hospital. While there, she learned her boyfriend had sold most of her kitchen appliances. By the time she got back, he was busy loading her shack onto the back of a truck. With the help of neighbours, they chased him away, but she was left with nothing."

I shook my head as Brian continued.

"As I said, Rosie is a remarkable woman and she vowed to start over. With donated equipment, her kitchen was soon up and running again. There are now over fifty such kitchens in Cape Town."

While enjoying my second beer, I reflected on what I had seen that day and realised my image of the townships had irrevocably changed. Before, they had been places of violence, but that was largely in the past. No question, Khayelitsha was still a tough place. The vast majority of its residents are trying to get by and provide for their children, surviving any way they can.

Robben Island

'Journeying to Robben Island was like going to another country, its isolation made it not simply another prison, but a world of its own.' — Nelson Mandela, Long Walk to Freedom

From the moment I awoke, it was a race against time. I glanced at my watch before cursing and leaping from my bunk. Mr. Smelly Feet snored contentedly, his pungent feet protruding from the sheets. I blasted some deodorant in his general direction before bolting for the door.

I caught a local bus to the sparkling Victoria & Albert Waterfront. This is Cape Town's tourist trap, where the visitor can feel as if they never left their Western comforts. Everything you need is there, including five-star hotels, Starbucks, Hard Rock Café and overpriced diamond stores. In short, if you had no interest in seeing anything of Cape Town or South Africa, this would be the place for you.

I nervously glanced at my watch and noticed with horror it was five minutes to ten. After getting off the bus, I sprinted through the glitzy waterfront shopping complex. With a minute to spare, I breathlessly boarded the only transport that day bound for Robben Island.

Robben Island is a sandy spit of land in Table Bay. Since Europeans first arrived, it has been used as a place of exile, a prison, a leper colony and then a prison again. Upon disembarking, I boarded the bus with the other passengers that took us to the prison.

We entered the penitentiary through a gateway that bore the inscription 'Robben Island – We Serve with Pride.' Large strips of paint peeled from the sign and I was a little surprised the current authorities allowed it to remain. Maybe they did so to let it to fade and rot, like the system it once represented.

Our prison guide was ideally qualified to lead the tour, having spent five years as an inmate on the island. Derick Basson had been convicted of sabotage after burning down a rent office and sent to Robben Island.

"I should only have been charged with the lesser offense of arson but the authorities wanted a greater sentence for me," he told us. A slight man of about fifty years, he spoke with a gentle voice that betrayed no trace of bitterness.

Derick led us outside to the prison yard, surrounded by a high wall. We gathered around an information display, highlighted by a black and white photograph taken in 1964 of shackled prisoners sitting in two lines in that same yard. One line of men broke rocks with small hammers while the others sewed clothing. Prison guards walked behind them, making sure the pace of work never slowed. It was a picture of despair. Only a man as positive as Mandela could write about that same yard,

'Some mornings I walked out into the courtyard and every living thing there, the seagulls and wagtails, the small trees, and even the stray blades of grass seemed to smile and shine in the sun. It was at such times, when I perceived the beauty of even this small, closed-in corner of the world, that I knew that someday my people and I would be free.' — Nelson Mandela, *Long Walk to Freedom*

Inside the prison, we were shown the cell where Mandela spent much of his adult life. His prisoner number is now almost as famous as his name — 466/64, the 466th prisoner admitted in 1964. Unlike the metal bed on display in his former cell, when he first arrived he had to sleep on a straw mat on the ground. I peeped out the small window of his cell, which looked out over the exercise yard. This was his view of the world for the eighteen years he spent on Robben Island. From that tiny cell, he formulated his thoughts on the future of his country. I felt humbled to share the same space he had, even for a few short moments.

"Black prisoners were called boys by the prison authorities and forced to wear shorts, usually worn by children," Derick told us. "They also received only one cube of sugar, while coloured prisoners got two. Black prisoners also got only half the allowance of meat, fish, tea and coffee that coloured and Indian prisoners were entitled to."

"Was this the same for Mandela?" a member of the tour group asked.

"Yes, he was treated the same way," replied Derick. "Like the other prisoners, Mandela was only allowed one letter every six months and only one visit. The authorities censored newspapers and letters so heavily that when you got them, they were unreadable. They didn't speak our African languages and so anything they didn't understand, they cut out."

What our guide did not add was that, while in prison, Mandela lost his son in a car crash, his mother to natural causes and the authorities refused to allow him attend either funeral. He also suffered permanent eye damage while being forced to work in the nearby lime quarry.

Those blows would have drowned any other man in bitterness and despair. Mandela later told how, in moments of doubt and weakness, he drew great strength from the poem *Invictus*, written by William Ernest Henley.

The poet was a man who could certainly sympathise with Mandela's brief moments of despair. Henley contracted tuberculosis of the bone when he was just twelve years old. He suffered from the disease until he was twenty-five but, by that time, it had progressed to both his feet. The doctors told him they would have to remove his severely infected leg immediately and that, if he were to survive, they would need to remove the other one as well. A strong-willed person, he gave the doctors permission to remove one leg, but insisted on keeping the other.

In 1875, from his hospital bed, he wrote *Invictus*, Latin for undefeated. It was the perfect response to the challenges of life.

Mandela recited the poem to himself and other prisoners as a way to bolster their spirits, motivating them to press onward. Despite the succession of injustices he suffered, Mandela felt empowered by the poem's message of self-mastery and refused to bow his head. After nearly twenty years of study, he obtained a distance-learning law degree from the University of London in 1988. Along with other prisoners, he founded Robben Island University, where prisoners shared knowledge through lectures. He even learned Afrikaans to bolster relations with the prison guards.

Leaving the prison, we boarded the bus again for a short tour of the island where, to my amazement, I saw penguins. Some heartless naturalist had named them jackass penguins, as their call sounds very much like a donkey. I never heard it to verify, however. The driver pointed to a small graveyard, containing the dead of the long-disbanded leper colony. We had a brief stop at the lime quarry where Mandela damaged his eyesight before leaving the island.

Even though it was where Mandela and others endured years of unjust imprisonment, Robben Island is now a monument to the victory of forgiveness over revenge. After what he had suffered, the man released in 1990 after 26 years in prison was not a bitter, hate-filled terrorist. He was instead a man who preached forgiveness and reconciliation. He even invited his former prison warders to his presidential inauguration ceremony. His message of reconciliation helped keep the country together during those crucial years after the end of white rule, forging a new South Africa. Against the odds, Mandela had won the final victory. He had overcome. He was *Invictus*.

Invictus

Out of the night that covers me,
Black as the Pit from pole to pole,
I thank whatever gods may be
For my unconquerable soul.

In the fell clutch of circumstance
I have not winced nor cried aloud.
Under the bludgeonings of chance
My head is bloody, but unbowed.

Beyond this place of wrath and tears
Looms but the Horror of the shade,
And yet the menace of the years
Finds, and shall find, me unafraid.

It matters not how strait the gate,
How charged with punishments the scroll,
I am the master of my fate:
I am the captain of my soul.
— William Ernest Henley

Climbing Table Mountain

Regardless of where I had gone in Cape Town – District Six, Robben Island, Khayelitsha – the one common factor was Table Mountain. It was visible no matter where I went in the city. Each day, it seemed to call to me, tempting me to explore its delicious contours. No matter what historic changes each passing decade brought to the city streets below, the Mountain stood aloof, like an ancient African elephant paying scant regard to the ants scuttling at its feet. It offered peace and calm from the busy city life. It was time for me to answer its call.

On my last day in Cape Town, I caught a motorised rickshaw, known as a *rikki*, from the hostel. It zipped past the very tempting cable-car station on Tafelberg Road before stopping a few hundred metres beyond. This was the start of Platteklip Gorge, the most direct hiking route to the summit. The vast majority of the mountain's nearly 800,000 annual visitors choose the cable car, but I decided to ignore that in favour of some much-needed exercise. With sandwiches and a bottle of water in my backpack, I started upwards.

My early morning start meant I was mercifully cloaked in shade for the first part of the hike. The surrounding scrubs and gum trees also added to the shady environs. The gravel path soon became a series of stone steps that would eventually lead me to the top of the mountain. Platteklip Gorge was the most direct route and, not surprisingly, the most strenuous. The three kilometres to the summit rose over seven hundred meters and was sure to test my leg muscles.

With sweat dripping steadily from my forehead, I paused to watch the silver capsule of the cable car gliding overhead with its cargo of tourists. Suddenly, it didn't seem like such a bad way to get to the top. I swallowed a few mouthfuls of water before grimacing and pressing onward.

I wondered if António de Saldanha had found the going so hard when he became the first European to climb Table Mountain by the same route in 1503. I'm sure he had more pressing business to tend to after landing at Table Bay, but such is the draw of this magnificent peak that he indulged in a spot of hiking instead.

Table Mountain is old, six times older than the Himalayas and five times as old as the Rockies. It is also home to such a diverse range of plant life you get the idea this is no mere mountain, more like a living eco-system.

Now, anyone who knows me will be aware I don't have much interest in botany. You will never catch me squatting over a tiny, pink flower with a magnifying glass in hand, whistling in amazement. That said, I couldn't help but be impressed by the sheer range of plant life on Table Mountain. It is home to more varieties of fern than there are in the entire United Kingdom. The Cape forms one of the planet's six floral Kingdoms, but more about that later.

About thirty minutes into my hike, the sun appeared over Devil's Peak and flooded the valley with light. As the sun beat down on my head and neck, I cursed myself for forgetting my sunblock.

As I rested against a rock to catch my breath, a group of school kids on a class outing passed by. They were in a boisterous mood, singing and joking, as a few teachers led the way, grimacing with effort. A little later, a leotard-clad jogger overtook me heading up the mountain. I was amazed and slightly humbled at such fitness as I struggled onwards. The path rose high above the city and I stopped frequently to admire the view and take water.

A few hundred meters from the top, I entered a deep cleft in the mountain. Table Bay slowly disappeared from view, as I made my way between the towering mountain walls. An hour after starting, I emerged on the flat plateau of Table Mountain. Panting and wheezing, I leaned on my knees for a minute to catch my breath before surveying my surroundings. A welcome breeze soon forced me to change my sodden t-shirt. Refreshed, I started walking across the mountain toward the cable car terminus.

I ambled along the corrugated surface of the

mountaintop until I reached the Head, a popular viewpoint where the cable car terminates. From there, I enjoyed the panoramic majesty of Cape Town, Robben Island and the ocean beyond, dotted with a flotilla of ships and pleasure crafts. Little chipmunk-like creatures called rock dassies scrambled over rubbish bins and feasted on leftover food. They were so tame that one of them ate some peanuts from my hand. Incredibly, the closest living relation to these little creatures is the elephant. A more mismatched pair of cousins, I couldn't imagine.

Sitting on a stone wall with a soft drink, I remembered when I'd first seen a picture of Table Mountain. My mother had given me an illustrated atlas of the world for my thirteenth birthday. I spent hours browsing its pages, the same way many other boys my age read football magazines. Magical names of far-flung places such as Zanzibar, Casablanca, Lhasa, Cape Town and Beijing danced in my mind. They sounded like places from a fairy tale.

I especially remembered looking at a picture of Cape Town with Table Mountain in the background and thinking, *what an incredible looking mountain. What would it be like to walk along the streets of that city and meet its people? Was Table Mountain flat like a real table?*

I was delighted to have realised my dream of seeing Cape Town and standing on its fabled mountain. However, it also saddened me a little. Cape Town and its illustrious mountain would never again hold the same mysterious beauty that only the mind can conceive. Vivid memories and colour photographs had replaced my magical image of the city. Cape Town had been a fantastic start to my South African odyssey and I couldn't wait to see more of the country.

Before returning to the city via cable car, I looked down the coast towards Cape Point and the Garden Route beyond. There, an encounter awaited me that I had been both dreading and anticipating since I started planning the trip.

It would wait no longer.

3 THE GARDEN ROUTE

*'You go inside the cage, cage goes in the water, you go in
the water, shark's in the water ... our shark. Farewell
and adieu to you fair Spanish ladies...'*

*- Quint to Hooper when Hooper brings his shark cage on
board the Orca (from the film JAWS)*

Shark Cage Diving

Despite the warm weather at sea that day, I was
shaking like a leaf. I had just watched a Great
White shark leap from the water with its jaws
agape, displaying rows of razor-sharp teeth. I was
now being asked to slide into a metal shark cage
that looked as secure as a shopping trolley while
sharks patrolled the water below. Considering I

have an acute fear of being eaten alive made this even crazier.

Why was I doing this?

Ever since I watched the film, JAWS, as an impressionable ten-year-old, I've had a healthy fear of the Great White shark. After watching what the man-eating star of that film did made me forever cautious when swimming in the sea. Despite my anxiety, something drew me to these creatures, so I decided to go and see if they were as fierce as I feared.

What better place to look than in South Africa.

The small fishing village of Gansbaai is only a two-hour drive from Cape Town. Dyer and Geyser Islands, just off the coast, are home to a large colony of over fifty thousand seals and, as a result, a favourite feeding ground for Great Whites. The deep channel between these two islands is known as Shark Alley and is acknowledged as one of the best places in the world to view the Great White. Boating companies run daily trips to Shark Alley and shark cage diving has turned this small, sleepy village into a mecca for thrill-seekers.

Piet Smal has been running shark cage diving trips for years and appeared in many documentaries featuring the Great White. His knowledge and understanding of this ancient predator made him an ideal guide.

Before setting out to sea that day, we enjoyed a

light breakfast while Piet held a safety briefing.

"You are not allowed to jump into the water or try to 'bond' with the sharks, no matter how friendly they seem," Piet told us, to a ripple of disbelieving laughter.

"Believe me, I've seen it happen," he said, deadly serious.

What kind of fruitcake would want to jump into the water with Great Whites, I wondered?

Afterwards, everyone had to sign an unsettling legal waiver of the type, "I will not press charges if I get an arm or leg bitten off..." Not what my nerves needed. We finally boarded the well-equipped cruiser and, with seagulls swirling above us, chugged out of the harbour in search of JAWS.

After thirty minutes or so, the crew found a good spot and dropped anchor. In order to attract the sharks, Piet laced the water with a mixture of fish guts and sardines called chum. The Great White's acute sense of smell can detect blood in the water from over five kilometres away. It didn't take long for the first of the distinctive dorsal fins to appear. Four sharks circled the boat, the largest of them being about four meters long and, according to Piet, well over two tonnes in weight.

Piet attached a rope to a large tuna head and threw it into the water. As soon as a shark struck, Piet pulled the tuna head away, giving us the chance to photograph the shark with its jaws wide open.

"We're not allowed to feed the sharks, only bait them," Piet explained. A member of the crew then cast a seal-shaped decoy into the water. One shark circled the decoy cautiously for a few minutes before unleashing its attack. The Great White has several rows of over three thousand teeth and made good use of them all as it tore at the decoy. We swallowed hard at the sight of the Great White in action.

"Right," Piet smiled, "time for you lot to get in the cage".

My moment of truth had arrived.

As I squeezed into my wetsuit, the crew lowered the flimsy-looking cage into the water. The cylindrical cage could accommodate two people at a time and was secured to the boat with ropes and floatation barrels. A shark could easily jump into the cage, I observed. Piet threw some chum nearby and beckoned the first volunteers to approach. I knew watching others in the cage would only make me more nervous so, with wobbly knees, I stepped forward.

"Don't worry," Piet said, "The shark may brush its nose against the cage, but it'll never attack it. They're just curious."

Yeah, right, I thought, as I adjusted my mask. My heart pounded like never before as I slid into the cage alongside another brave soul. No sooner had I done so than Piet shouted, "Dive." Taking a deep breath, I eased myself under the water. My feet found the floor of the cage just in time to see a Great White loom out of the shadows. By reflex, I recoiled at the sight, forcing myself to the back of the cage. It swam by slowly and seemed to be completely oblivious to our presence. My cage buddy had thought to bring a disposable underwater camera and was busy taking photographs. I was too busy trying to keep my hands and feet inside the cage to worry about photography. After surfacing for air, I dove down again and all my nerves evaporated. To see this ancient creature up close was a truly amazing experience. It glided with an absolute minimum of effort. It was magical, beautiful, and about to become scary.

After I surfaced for air, Piet shouted at me to dive down again and look straight ahead. I followed his instructions in time to see another shark swim past me with the same effortless ease as before. Suddenly, it turned and headed straight for the cage. With jaws agape and showing rows of its deadly teeth, the shark brushed its nose against the cage before swimming away. I nearly let my bladder go at that point. Oh, who am I kidding, I *did* leave it go. There was a bloody shark poking its nose into my cage. You would have done the same, believe me.

I burst to the surface like a cork with the rest of

the boat gasping at what had just happened. By the time Piet helped me back on board, I was smiling broadly. Despite my fear, I was thrilled by my close encounter with the Great White and I wanted more. I got back into the cage twice more that day and continued to marvel at those amazing creatures of the sea.

As the trip ended and we sped towards shore, I felt thrilled to have finally made the acquaintance of the Great White. It was not the man-eating monster of the movies but one of the oldest creatures on earth and one of nature's finest, most perfect creations. My fear had finally disappeared and been replaced by respect.

Still, I don't think I'll be swimming near Shark Alley in the near future. Just out of respect, of course.

Hermanus

Once safely back on dry land, I relaxed and strolled around the charming town of Hermanus. Everything on display in the brightly coloured gift shops along the sea front seemed to be connected to sharks or, the other great draw, whales. Between June and December, this is probably the best place in the world to view the migration of southern right whales. No need for boats, as the whales can be seen breaching just offshore.

Further out to sea, you can also witness another

of nature's great spectacles – the sardine run. After spawning between May and July, billions of sardines move up the South African coast towards warmer waters. The shoals can be up to seven kilometres long and two kilometres wide. As the sardines migrate, the sea literally boils with predators. Dolphins, sharks, whales and birds – even penguins – all converge on this mass migration to feed. All this sea-based activity is a huge tourist draw and deserves its catchy motto as 'the greatest shoal on earth'.

I was staying at the friendly Moby Backpackers near the town centre. The hostel was conveniently attached to a nice bar, which I visited later that evening after my shark-diving experience. As I chatted to the barman, a customer walked in with two dogs. One was a huge Great Dane and the other a little terrier. The terrier jumped up onto a barstool and popped his chin on the counter. His owner ordered two beers and poured one into a metal dish for the Great Dane. The little terrier, sadly, got nothing for his troubles. I tried to make some small talk, as both dog and owner slurped their beers. He was thin and deeply tanned with a greying moustache. He told me he was retired and I asked him what he did before.

"I was a policeman, busy trying to keep the blacks in check," he smiled thinly. "Those bloody terrorists are in power now, hard to believe it." There was hatred in every word he uttered. It unnerved me to be sitting beside someone so filled with rage. I drained my glass and left.

Having access to a bar was not the only bonus of Moby's. I was also lucky enough to have access to great food. Stuart 'Stuey' McDonald was the hostel cook. A champion chef in his native Scotland, he was cooking his way around the world. While talking to him at the bar, I discovered he was serving his famous marinated filet mignon the following evening.

"This is my speciality," he assured me. When he told me it was fifty rand, I balked. That was steep by local standards, although very cheap compared to a similar meal in Ireland. He convinced me to sign up for one. When I told him I wanted it cooked well-done, he shook his head.

"Trust me, you want it medium-rare," he said, marking this down without bothering to consult me. Boy, was he right. The steak I enjoyed the following evening was the nicest I ever tasted. 'Melt-in-your-mouth' finally had real meaning.

Once I had been shark diving and steak eating, there wasn't much to hold me in Hermanus so I booked a place on the Baz Bus to my next destination. The 'Baz' is a bus service dedicated to carrying backpackers around South Africa. Unlike public transport, pickups and drop-offs are from the door of your current accommodation to the door of your next one. This is great for the safety-conscious, but unfortunately limits the places you can visit.

I left Hermanus the following morning on the Baz, bound for Knysna on the Garden Route. On board, I got chatting with Allen from New York and Amy from England. Allen told me about his extensive travels around the world and I listened to his stories with keen interest. We clicked instantly and I managed to convince them both to stop at Knysna instead of their intended destination of Wilderness.

Known as the pearl of the Garden Route, Knysna sits on an impressive lagoon, mantled by indigenous forests extending into Tsitsikamma National Park. The following morning, we rented bikes from the hostel and cycled to the Knysna Heads, two pillars of rock standing guard at the lagoon entrance. The safe waters of the natural harbour made the town an important port for shipbuilding in the 1800s and provided easy access to vast woods that were exploited for timber used in shipbuilding. The forests were once home to a large herd of elephants, of which only three remain.

It was a wet day and cycling was tough going with some steep climbs. We eventually got to the entrance of the lagoon where there was a small lighthouse. The sea churned angrily, whipped up by a strong wind. After getting soaked by yet another heavy shower, the three of us turned to cycle back to the hostel.

Later that evening, we headed out for a few drinks to a local club called Zanzibar. There was an unusual clientele there that evening to say the least. Men danced around the bar dressed in pink tutus, while others strutted in black leather pants somehow missing the rear end. It turned out to be Pink Week in the town, an event that attracts thousands of cross-dressers, gays and lesbians. Not a great place for any single guys looking for girls, as you can imagine.

With Pink Week in full swing, I left Knysna the following day and agreed to meet up with Allen and Amy further along the route. The Baz Bus dropped me off at a hostel near the remote Storm's River. I was there for one reason only – the bungee jump at Bloukrans Bridge.

Bungee Jump

When I saw the bridge the following morning, I swallowed hard. It spanned a yawning gorge and seemed much higher that its 216 meters. A jump from that height would be like taking the lift to the 70th floor of a building before taking a swan dive off the windowsill.

At the reception, everyone had to be weighed before being allowed to jump. I was taken aback when I weighed in at a hefty hundred and eighty pounds.

Damn you, Castle Beer.

Next, I had to sign another liability waiver similar to what I had done for the shark cage diving. As I scribbled my name to the bottom of the page, I thought it was funny how both shark cage diving and bungee jumping can involve loss of limbs and excruciating death. Before departing toward the bridge, I looked up at the Guinness Book of Records sign, declaring it the highest bungee jump in the world. Walking toward the jump area, I stared down into the distant river below. It seemed miles away and I had second thoughts about the whole thing. It went against every part of my being to do this.

I was the first to jump that day and felt it was better to get it over with before I lost my nerve. The whole process felt like a death-row prisoner being prepared for the electric chair. Two members of the jump crew went through the series of straps and buckles attached to me, double-checking each one in quick succession. I tried to relax by cracking a few jokes, but it was pure gallows humour. One of the crew was a pony-tailed cool dude who smiled silently at my gags. He had seen it all before, the attempts to remain calm before taking the plunge.

"Because this is the highest bungee jump in the world, everyone has to wear a harness as well as having your ankles bound," Cool Dude said. "Remember to walk out onto the platform and look forward, not down. We will give you a countdown of five and on five, spread your arms in the air and do your best Superman impression. Do not jump after five, jump on…"

His final instructions were drowned out by the sound of my racing heart. With my feet tightly bound and attached to a harness across my shoulders and stomach, they stood me up. My knees went a little as I shuffled towards the narrow platform above the abyss. They each grabbed one of my arms and extended it out from my body. They then let go and stepped back off the platform. I was on my own.

I could back out now, I thought briefly. *No one would mind and I would never see these people again.* Before I could entertain the thought any further, I leaned forward, feeling my feet leave the firmness of the bridge.

I jumped.

I leapt.

I flew.

It was all over in seconds – the fall, the screaming, the tightening, the bouncing up and down and the swinging. Once I slowed down a bit, I whooped with delight. In that upside-down position, my eyes filled with water and I couldn't see much. Dangling a few hundred feet above the river, I had to wait for someone to come and hoist me back up.

Nobody tells you about the waiting. Those minutes I spent dangling in mid-air felt like an hour. I became convinced my boots were slowly slipping off and the harness was coming loose. I prayed for them to hurry.

"I'm coming down to get you," were the sweetest words I'd heard in ages, as one of the guys abseiled down and hooked himself onto me. We were both hauled onto that blessed bridge and boy, was I relieved to be back on solid ground again. I walked back to the reception on a cloud of air, high on adrenaline for the rest of the day.

Tsitsikamma National Park

The next day, the owners of the hostel dropped me off at Tsitsikamma National Park. Remember I said I was going to talk about the Cape Floral Kingdom? Tsitsikamma National Park is in the heart of this kingdom, one of six on the planet and by far the smallest. However, size really does not matter in this case. According to UNESCO, The Cape Floral Kingdom represents less than 0.5% of the area of Africa, but is home to nearly 20% of the continent's flora, including fynbos, hardy plants with wooden stems and fine leaves. Of this vast range of plant life, 70% occur nowhere else on earth. The diversity and concentration of flora within an area the size of Portugal is truly astounding.

I started on the three-hour Waterfall Trail, part

of the much longer five-day Otter Trail. The walk
started out easily enough, following yellow arrows
on a well-marked path, but that only lulled me into
a false sense of security. After about 500 meters, the
yellow arrows left the path and wandered across
huge rocks along the shore. For the next few
kilometres, I scrambled over slippery boulders,
climbed stone steps and, at one point, inched along
a narrow cliff face. After a lot of climbing and
boulder hopping, I finally arrived at a lovely
waterfall, cascading down a series of rocks into a
clear pool.

Further along, I approached the aptly named
Storms River Suspension Bridge. The sea was white
with anger that day and, from a distance, it looked
as if the bridge spanned a liquid glacier of frothing
foam. After crossing the wooden bridge, I endured
a tough walk up the opposite hill to the lookout
post, which afforded fine views of wild forest and
sea. Returning to the hostel soon after, I readied
myself for city life once more.

Crossing Storms River Suspension Bridge

Port Elizabeth — The Friendly City

The logos of Ford, General Motors and Volkswagen dominated the sprawling industrial complex on the outskirts of Port Elizabeth. That first glimpse of the city didn't promise much, but those hideous buildings soon gave way to a lovely beachfront.

I booked into a hostel and wasted little time organising a township tour. A Swiss girl, Sandra, joined me as the tour guide collected us later that evening. We were the only ones on the tour that day. Sandra made little reply to my questions about her travels. She seemed quiet and serious, staring out the bus window the whole time.

Our driver told us the local township residents had suffered the same forced relocations as those in

Cape Town after the infamous Group Areas Act came into force. He pointed out the police station where Steve Biko, the black anti-apartheid activist, was interrogated and tortured by the police in 1977. Biko was later transported to Pretoria, where he died of his injuries.

"The entire township has been surveyed and rezoned so that every home has access to running water and electricity," he told us proudly. "You'll get a chance to see it all later."

We had tea at our driver's home before a local man named Mdondo arrived to take us on the walking part of the tour. He smelled of beer and slurred as he spoke and our host didn't seem very impressed with his appearance. Despite his misgivings, he had little choice but allow him to lead us through the Port Elizabeth Township.

Mdondo was tall with impressive shoulder-length dreadlocks and a French-style moustache and goatee. As we followed him through the township, we encountered girls singing and children playing. We visited a *spaza*, or township store, and talked openly with the locals. This was exactly the kind of interaction the Cape Town tour did not have. While we spent most of our time looking out a van window in Cape Town, here we mixed with people and really experienced township life.

"You must come home with me and visit my

wife and children," Mdondo insisted, leading us swiftly through a maze of shacks until opening a creaking door. Inside, flattened cardboard boxes covered the walls. He woke his wife and two children, who slept in the same bed. While his younger son was shy of these late-evening visitors, the other boy relished the interruption. He had short, spiky hair and a winning smile, sporting a stud earring in his left ear. Wearing a bright, yellow jumper, he posed for photos and laughed when I ruffled his hair.

Mdondo with his family

Mdondo's wife stayed in bed during our visit, wearing an orange, woollen hat. It was winter in South Africa and, while warm during the day, it became much cooler at night. I felt like an intruder, but it was interesting to see inside of a township shack. Even though he was poor, Mdondo was proud of his family home, however uncertain his future. Despite my initial misgivings, I warmed to Mdondo. He was just a man with a family, trying to get by the best way he could.

We returned to the driver's house where we ate supper before visiting the local Coleman's shebeen for a few beers. I challenged another patron to a game of pool, losing badly. Mdondo introduced me to a friend of his wearing a blue t-shirt with *Norway* stretched across his very considerable bulk. Mdondo told me his friend was a member of the African National Congress (ANC), the dominant political party in South Africa. Mdondo pulled Sandra into the conversation.

"Is there much being done to help people still living in shacks and awaiting new housing?" Sandra asked him.

"Yes, but there is so much more to do. Apartheid left a huge mark on the country and this will not be fixed overnight," he said, shaking his head before taking a great swallow from his bottle. "We ask the people to be patient with us."

"Do you hold any bad feeling towards the white people for this?" she asked. He smiled and shook his head again.

"No, no, not at all. That is all in the past. Madiba

[an affectionate term for Nelson Mandela] said we must forgive those who wronged us."

I suddenly remembered a passage in Mandela's book and tried hard to remember it correctly. Clearing my throat, I added, "Mandela also said you must forgive those who wronged you or else you will never be free. This is true but also a very hard thing to do. Mandela did it and you did it. Truly, South Africa's wealth comes not from its gold or diamonds but from people like you."

On hearing that, the ANC man uttered something in Xhosa to Mdondo and wrapped his great arms around me in a bear hug, causing me to spill my beer. Port Elizabeth truly deserves its moniker, the Friendly City.

Back at the hostel, I had a nagging feeling that my travels had not yet begun. Everything had been easy so far, too easy. Despite its undeniable beauty, I felt the Garden Route was missing something. The towns were lovely, the beaches clean, and the shops sparkling but I was travelling through an African country without seeing many black people. At times, I felt as if I was walking through a film set with the crew and many of the actors kept out of the scenes. They did wander into view at times, in a shop, driving down a street or cleaning a window but they seemed notably absent considering they made up over eighty percent of the population.

All that was about to change.

4 INTO AFRICA

Hogsback

As I watched the passing landscape from the bus window, there was little doubt I had left the Garden Route. The land was bare and devoid of vegetation with hardly a tree in sight. Native kraals dotted the countryside while goats, cattle and women carrying huge bundles on their heads wandered along the road. This was the first time in South Africa I had seen typically 'African' scenery.

Reading back on my travel journal from that day, I realised it was a strange comment to make. Up to now, I had not considered anything I had seen to be 'African' because it was different to what I expected Africa to be. The current landscape better matched my stereotypical view of the entire continent; chickens running about on a dusty road, half-naked children waving at our passing bus and poorly dressed people living in straw huts.

The area I passed through was the Eastern Cape, the poorest of South Africa's provinces. It was created out of the former Xhosa homelands of Ciskei and Transkei. The Xhosa number over eight million and theirs is the second most spoken language in South Africa after Zulu.

The former apartheid government came up with the idea of the homelands in order to create 'independent' states where the various tribes could call home. This 'Bantustan' policy sought to assign every black citizen to a 'homeland' according to his or her ethnic identity. Ten homelands were created in this fashion to rid South Africa of its black citizens, opening the way for mass forced removals.

On paper, the homelands operated like a sovereign state. They had their own postage stamps, police and parliaments. In reality, however, they were merely puppet states of apartheid South Africa. The homelands were poor and overcrowded, thus forcing people to seek work in the cities of South Africa. The government viewed these migrant workers as foreigners and forced them to carry passbooks at all times. This was all engineered to keep whites in power and to retain the best land for themselves.

After a short break in East London, I endured a tiring two-hour bus journey to Hogsback along torturous, winding roads. Tucked away deep in the

Amatola Mountains, this village has a reputation of being a magical place. Perched high above the Tyume Valley, Hogsback is clustered along a single stretch of road. Surrounded by centuries-old indigenous forests, the name Hogsback comes from the surrounding hills, which resemble the bristled back of a hog.

I read somewhere that the renowned South African born writer, JRR Tolkien, was reputed to have visited the area before he wrote *Lord of the Rings*. The Amatola Forest, in particular, allegedly inspired his description of the Eden-like Middle Earth.

However tenuous the link, Hogsback has not been shy in promoting its association with the great writer. 'Camelot', 'Hobbiton', 'Rivendell', 'The Shire', 'Hobbit Lane' and 'Middle Earth' all appeared as place names in the magical village. Therefore, my choice of accommodation at 'Away with the Faeries' shouldn't raise too many eyebrows. Situated on top of a hill with spectacular views of the valley, it was rustic and perfect for those looking to relax and chill out. Hammocks swung between trees in the garden, while cosy fires encouraged reading in the sitting room.

Hogsback was certainly a place where you could chill out for days or even weeks and why not. One of the beauties of long-term travel is not having set goals and timetables to follow.

Fancy staying a few more days at an idyllic beach? No problem. Want to get the hell out of town in a hurry? Done. Too early to have a few drinks while lazing in a hammock? No way.

This is how travellers end up spending weeks and even months in one place. *If you are having fun and enjoying the company of the people around you, why go any further? Time is on your side.*

The next morning, I took a map from the hostel before setting off in search of Tolkien's Middle Earth. Before heading into the woods, I got chatting to Pat, a local resident who ran 4x4 tours of the area.

"That's some view," I said, admiring the sweep of the valley.

"Yea, I never get tired of it. It's really a special place," he replied.

Before I could continue, Pat interrupted. "Only thing wrong with the place is the lazy blacks. They're bad for the country, never do a day's work and only thieve off the state."

I hung my head and smiled weakly at his increasingly vicious tirade before making some lame excuse to leave. I walked the next few minutes with his voice ringing in my ears, his caustic comments taunting me. I had to stop and sit down on a grassy ditch at the edge of the valley.

Why had I not responded to him? Why had I not

informed him his views were outdated and racist? Why didn't I repeat one of Mandela's quotes from his book, such as *'No one is born hating another person because of the colour of his skin and if he can be taught to hate, he can be taught to love.'*

In the end, I felt I hadn't been in the country long enough to make such statements. Who am I to judge the white people and their opinions? I had only been in their country three weeks and could hardly lecture them about how to behave. Instead of being judgemental, I chose to listen to what people had to say, as much as I might disagree with their opinions.

Wandering along the earthen path, I delighted in the nature surrounding me. Ancient tree-roots snaked across moss-encrusted rocks and boulders, like the withered hand of a giant wizard. Along the way, cherry blossoms, rhododendrons, azaleas and lilies grew in abundance. A burst of green ferns, wet with tiny dewdrops, partially obscured the path, while alien-like fungi clung from decaying tree-stumps.

I stopped briefly at the Swallow Tail Falls and then Bridal Veil Falls. The ground was rich with leaves and twigs, snapping with each step. I stumbled over a fallen ivy-choked tree, slowly being reclaimed by the forest floor. I reached the Madonna and Child Falls, tumbling across a succession of rocks into a clear pool at the bottom. It was an idyllic place to rest and enjoy my lunch, accompanied by the gentle gurgling of the waterfall. Nearby, a single, magnificent shaft of sunlight illuminated a spot of forest floor, like a leaf-strewn stage being readied for an unseen cast.

It was easy to see why these woods might have inspired Tolkien to imagine a world filled with fantastic creatures. As I ate my cheese sandwiches, I got the feeling I was being watched. It's something peculiar to woods everywhere, the feeling there is someone — or something — is lurking behind a tree, watching you. It would be very easy to imagine Hobbits trampling through the lush greenery, going for a swim in a rock pool or making a home in some earthen mound.

After seeing the beauty of the hilltop, I decided to explore the lowlands the following day. I rented a bicycle at the hostel and freewheeled the hair-raising fifteen kilometres down to the village of Alice. I had to be on my guard for stray cattle wandering along the road. Local people let them graze along the grassy roadsides but they had a nasty habit of meandering across my path as I sped downhill. The brakes on my bicycle were worn and I had to veer wildly at times to avoid ploughing into those bovine roadblocks.

While whites dominated the village of Hogsback, the homes at the bottom of the valley were all black-owned. Traditional rondavels with circular walls and conical straw roofs sprinkled the hill slopes. Other homes were rectangular-shaped with a very rough finish of mud and clay, painted blue on one side only. Many had small gardens with vegetable rows. While they appeared poor, the local people at least enjoyed space that would be the envy of anybody living in a crowded township in Cape Town or Port Elizabeth.

As I rested on the bicycle handlebars, an old woman shuffled by carrying firewood on her head. A black scarf held her bundle together and she smiled as I took her photo.

Woman carrying firewood near Hogsback

I continued to a nearby shop and stopped to get a cold drink. The corrugated-iron building sat on a raised concrete platform and had a sign outside that read 'Upper Tyume'. A few posters decorated the outside wall advertising Lifebuoy Soap and

Kiwi Shoe Polish. I drank my cold soda on the front step, while kids approached me out of curiosity. A few of them took my bicycle for a ride while I chatted to some of the older ones.

I left them with a heavy heart, not because I hated leaving the delights of Alice, but because I dreaded the uphill journey ahead of me. I had just started my ascent when the bicycle chain slipped off. I dismounted to sort it out, only for the cursed thing to slip off again a few meters later. This happened about ten times before I finally broke down. I'm not proud of the language I used towards the poor bicycle that day, but my sanity was in serious danger.

The Lord obviously heard his name mentioned and decided to prevent further blasphemy. A passing pickup truck stopped and offered me a lift. I accepted before the driver could say another word and heaved the bicycle onto the flatbed before climbing aboard myself. As we ascended towards Hogsback, I could see why the hilltop retreat was so popular. With its cool climate and leafy woods, it was a tranquil piece of England in the heart of South Africa, a place where former British settlers could imagine they were home.

Umtata to Coffee Bay

After leaving Hogsback, my next port-of-call was the coastal resort town of Coffee Bay. On the Baz

Bus, I met up with Allen again who was going the same way. He introduced me to Warrick and Leanne, two fresh-faced English backpackers. We made a short stop at Mthatha, previously called Umtata when it was the capital of the Transkei. Unlike Hogsback, no whites were visible on the dusty streets. Roadside vendors sold roasted corn on sticks, while chickens flew across the road with their owner in chase.

Nelson Mandela grew up in the village of Qunu, not far from Mthatha. Steve Biko, Desmond Tutu and Thabo Mbeki were also raised in the Eastern Cape, commonly held to be the centre of the struggle for a democratic South Africa and the heartland of the ANC.

We were supposed to transfer to another bus bound for Coffee Bay, but were told it was full so the driver organised a local taxi-minibus to take us to our intended destination. We piled aboard but, ten miles outside Mthatha, one of the tyres blew. The driver didn't have a spare and had to flag down a lift back to town to get one, leaving the van parked on the hard shoulder of a lonely stretch of road.

With nothing to do, we got out of the van and walked around a bit. It was a fine evening, but our lengthening shadows told of the coming nightfall. The conical roofs of rondavels were visible a short way from the roadside. As we waited, local children materialized from the nearby fields of tall grass. They approached us shyly at first, curious about these white people stopped on the main road. We beckoned them to come closer. Someone offered them sweets and soon, we were playing chase with them, lifting any child I caught high above my head, much to their delight. They wore ragged clothes, peppered with patches. A distant voice called and the children suddenly waved goodbye to us, retreating into the tall grass from where they came.

Our driver arrived back soon after in another van.

"No problem," he beamed. "The spare wheel is under this van." After a frantic few minutes, however, the driver sadly informed us that the spare wheel was too rusty to remove. It was a comedy of errors at this stage, but nobody seemed to be the slightest bit worried. In fact, we were all enjoying this unexpected adventure.

Darkness fell an hour later and by that stage, we were anxious to get to Coffee Bay so decided to start hitchhiking. A woman with a pickup truck stopped and offered us a lift. Before climbing aboard, I noticed the floor of her pickup was littered with empty whiskey and gin bottles. I hesitated, but Allen, Warrick and Leanne accepted the lift without a second thought before disappearing into the night. The rest of us flagged down another woman who kindly offered to bring us to our destination. I sat beside her and thanked her profusely for stopping for us.

"The spirit told me to stop for you all," she informed me. "God will take care of us now." I nodded and wondered how long the journey would take. As we drove in the darkness, the headlights picked out people and cattle walking along the roadside. At times, we only narrowly avoided colliding with a stray cow along the dark road. I gripped the seat tightly with each near miss, expecting the next poor beast would not be so lucky.

Sure enough, a dog ran across the path of the car. Horribly, I realised it was too late for the car to brake. I flinched at the impact, the painful squeal of the animal and the sudden bump as the vehicle rolled over its body. One of the girls in the back screamed, but our driver didn't bat an eyelid.

"Another spirit into the Lord's bosom," she said, without taking her eyes off the road. The impact did some damage to the engine as the car shuddered to a halt outside the Coffee Shack Hostel. We had a quick whip-around and gave her some money towards the repairs. It had been some journey.

Coffee Bay Tour

Along with Allen and Warrick, I joined a tour of Coffee Bay the next day, visiting some of the local Transkei villages along the hilltops. Our guide,

Max, met us in the hostel before the tour started. We made our way up the gentle slopes surrounding Coffee Bay before reaching the top of a hilly ridge. To the north and west, rondavels dotted the rolling hills, painted various hues of blue. Cows bellowed in distant fields that fell away towards the vast expanse of the Indian Ocean.

"The bricks used to make local huts are made from a mixture of soil, grass, and cow shit," Max told us with obvious glee at the last ingredient. We passed women transporting large bundles of wheat or barley on their heads. Once we reached the first village, we visited a hut where an old woman demonstrated how to make flour, rolling a cigar-shaped stone over corn inside a shallow plinth. The flour is used to make bread and traditional African beer.

Max brought us to the hut of a *sangoma*, or traditional healer. Drawing back the ripped tarp covering the doorway, he ushered us inside. There sat an old woman with long, thin fingers and deeply wrinkled skin, dressed in an assortment of rags. Smoke from her open fire stung my eyes, as Max distributed some upturned buckets for us to sit on. She paid scant regard to us, as Max spoke to her in the clicking language of Xhosa. I noticed rows of jars behind her, filled with leaves and twigs of unknown origin. She muttered to herself as she fed the fire with pieces of dry wood.

"Does anyone have a health problem they need

a cure for?" Max asked. Nobody said a word until Warrick cleared his throat.

"Do you have anything for hangovers?" he asked tentatively. Max translated and the old witch nodded before taking some bark from one of her jars. She crushed it into a sheet of paper, folded it and presented to Warrick. He regarded it with curiosity. "How do I, ehm, take it?" he asked.

"Put it in hot water and drink it before your night out. It will be a big help," smiled Max. Warrick nodded and placed the dubious medicine in his pocket. Max leaned forward and whispered, "Fifty rand for the doctor please." Warrick balked when he heard the price, the same amount I had paid days earlier for the best steak I ever ate. However, it was not the time or place to argue and Warrick grudgingly pressed the money into the witchdoctor's grubby hand.

"Have you all heard the Xhosa clicking language before?" Max asked us as we ate a lunch of sampa and beans, the staple diet of most South Africans. We shook our heads. "Listen," said Max before uttering a series of rapid tongue clicks, some high and some low pitch. Up to that point, I would have said Mandarin was the hardest language in the world to master but after hearing Xhosa, I knew I was wrong.

After lunch, I asked Max where local people bury their dead. "We don't use cemeteries like people in the West," he said. "When the old people die, they are buried near the home." He told me his people worship their ancestors.

We then visited an isolated rondavel where we found a young boy. He had been recently circumcised and his face was covered in white clay, with only a rough blanket covering his body. Max spoke to him briefly in Xhosa before explaining the boy was a twenty-one-year-old *Abakhwetha*, an initiate who was undergoing the rite of passage from boyhood to manhood.

Boy undergoing his initiation into manhood

"The boy spends several weeks away from the village and is forbidden to see women during that time," Max explained. The circumcision is done in the bush, without anaesthetic or medical supplies, and infection is common. This traditional ceremony also involved education and survival in a hostile environment and is still an important part of life in this part of the world. Mandela described the importance of this ritual:

'When I was sixteen, the regent decided that it was time that I became a man. In Xhosa tradition, this is achieved through one means only: circumcision. In my tradition, an uncircumcised male cannot be heir to his father's wealth, cannot marry or officiate in tribal rituals. An uncircumcised Xhosa man is a contradiction in terms, for he is not considered a man at all, but a boy. For the Xhosa people, circumcision represents the formal incorporation of males into society. It is not just a surgical procedure, but a lengthy and elaborate ritual in preparation for manhood. As a Xhosa, I count my years as a man from the date of my circumcision.' — Nelson Mandela, Long Walk to Freedom

I also noticed that the boy in the hut held two sticks, which Mandela also mentioned in his book.

'I learned to stick-fight – essential knowledge to any rural African boy – and became adept at its various techniques, parrying blows, feinting in one direction and striking in another, breaking away from an opponent with quick footwork.'

In Xhosa culture, cows are the source of wealth. On the way to the local shebeen, Max told us if he wanted to marry a woman, he had to pay her family a lobolo, or 'bride price.' Marrying a teacher, for example, would set him back at least twenty cows. Upon arrival, I asked for a Castle beer but Max had other ideas.

"You must try our African beer, it's really good," he smiled. I consented and Max produced what seemed like a carton of milk from the fridge. He handed each of us a tin can filled with the milky liquid. We sat outside the shebeen on upturned crates and sampled the local brew. It was disgusting. It tasted more like sour milk and nothing like the beer I know and love. Made from maize and yeast, the concoction is known as *Umqombothi*, a word I assume means 'undrinkable.' I was certain each of us thought the same, but nobody wanted to offend Max. We smiled our approval and toasted to his good health.

As we sat there, a horse-drawn carriage passed by without a driver, as if commanded by a ghost. Allen asked Max if we should stop it but he shook his head before disappearing inside the shebeen. While he was gone, a bedraggled old woman approached our group holding a large can filled with beer. She muttered something before holding the can towards us. I was deeply touched by her act of generosity. Despite hating the stuff, I wasn't going to be rude and refuse this kind old lady. I mouthed my thanks and took the can, dividing the contents between us. She became very animated, shouting in Xhosa and shaking her fist at us. Max soon appeared and, after we explained what happened, he clapped his knees in laughter.

"Man, this old lady was not offering you her beer, she was *asking* for some of yours," he said, barely able to contain his laughter. "She is a beggar who collects old beer dregs from people in the village."

Almost in unison, we emptied the remaining beer onto the ground.

The Coffee Shack had a reputation for being a party hostel and it lived up to its billing later that evening. Allen and Warrick embarked on the infamous 'gauntlet', a drinking challenge that involved consuming twenty various alcoholic shots and cocktails. The boys pounded back each drink as it was presented, the pace slowing as the night wore on. Warrick gave up before the last drink, ripping his shirt off to display his hairy chest to the world. To his eternal credit, Allen completed the entire list of drinks to a huge round of applause from the bar.

"One last thing to do before we can add your name to the hall of fame," the devious barman said, tapping the blackboard behind him, "Twenty shots of beer."

Allen went pale at the idea but was up for the challenge. The barman brought a small table to the middle of the floor, where he sat a very groggy Allen and placed the tray of beer shots before him.

"To make this a little more interesting," he announced to the gathering crowd, "Allen will drink a shot of beer every time the line 'red light' is mentioned in this song."

With that, he pressed the play button on the stereo and The Police's *Roxanne* started. One of my fondest memories from South Africa is Allen pounded back beer after beer, surrounded by a crowd singing their hearts out to Roxanne. The thunderous applause after Allen downed the last shot of beer could be heard all the way to Cape Town.

Later, I found the shirtless Warrick asleep under a table and Leanne asked me to help her get him to bed. "Did you say the witchdoctor gave Warrick some cure for hangovers?" she asked, as we carried the lifeless Warrick out of the bar. "Hope he kept the receipt," she laughed.

With Allen and Warrick nursing monster hangovers the following morning, I went to see the famous 'Hole in the Wall', a natural sea-arch carved by the waves. Along the shore, local men dove off rocks before surfacing minutes later holding lobster-like fish. One wandered over to me with his catch, still squirming in his hand and dripping with water.

"Crayfish, you buy?" he asked.

I thanked him, but moved on up the shore. I hardly went ten feet before someone else offered me more crayfish. I bought a bag just to show the next seafood hawker I already had some. Up ahead, I could see the rock archway the sea had artfully carved, making it a tourist attraction. However lovely it appeared, it was also connected to one of the Xhosa nation's darkest hours.

By 1856, the Xhosa were in decline. The British had taken the lands of this once proud people, drought had withered their crops and their prized cattle were dying of a mysterious disease. Suddenly, hope appeared in the shape of a young girl named Nongqawuse. In February of that year, she claimed the spirits of her ancestors had spoken to her from a pool. They told her soldiers, who were incarnations of dead Xhosa warriors, would come onto land through the 'Hole in the Wall' on February 18 1857 and sweep the hated British into the sea. However, the Xhosa had to make a sacrifice to help the warriors by destroying their crops and killing their cattle, the source of their wealth as well as food. After the victory, there would be food in abundance for everybody, she promised. The Xhosa chief decided the visions were authentic and ordered his desperate people to obey them.

The allotted day dawned and nothing happened. By then, over 200,000 cattle had been slaughtered and all the summer crops burnt. Within a few months, more than a third of the entire Xhosa people had died of starvation and disease. It was easy for the British to take over the remnants of the tattered Xhosa kingdom and imprison the chiefs for their role in this 'genocide.' Nongqawuse spent the rest of her days in exile on Robben Island, leaving behind a shattered people.

I made my way back to the hostel with my bag of crayfish where I met a very bleary-eyed Allen.

"Feel like some food?" I joked, waving the bag in front of him. "Oh man, keep that away from me," he said, waving his arm. We made some coffee in the kitchen, as I recounted the night to him.

"I need to stop partying and get some exercise," he said, rubbing his head.

"Allen my friend," I said, toasting my coffee mug to his, "I have just the place in mind."

5 THE WILD COAST

Port St. Johns

During our final day in Coffee Bay, Allen and I agreed to do some hiking along the Wild Coast. We planned to take the Baz Bus to Mthatha and then a local minibus taxi to Port St. Johns. Minibus taxis are the cheapest and most popular form of transport in South Africa, carrying over 60% of the country's commuters. Used almost exclusively by the black population, they are also very dangerous. The drivers are notorious for running red lights, driving on the wrong side of the road and using vehicles in a perilous state of repair.

So it was no surprise I was nervous at the idea of taking one to Port St. Johns. We got directions to the taxi stop in Mthatha and joined the waiting passengers. When it arrived, Allen and I contorted ourselves into a seat meant for two alongside another man and his luggage. There didn't seem to be any organised stops, the driver stopped for people on the roadside whenever they raised their hands. At times, he careened around corners at speed, overtook traffic on blind turns and drove in a fashion that suggested he wanted to get off this planet in a hurry and take us all with him.

In spite of the driver's best efforts, we reached Port St. Johns in one piece. After getting off the bus, I took a few minutes to rub life back into my sore leg muscles before going in search of accommodation. The people in the area are ethnic Pondo, closely related to the Xhosa. We chose The Island Backpackers and, after getting settled in, returned to town for food and supplies. It was a small enough place, with most shops and stalls lining the main street. We were the only white people walking around and, even though people stopped to stare, nobody bothered us. We picked up some fruit, bottled water and other items for our planned hike along the Wild Coast.

Allen decided to take it easy the following day, but I had other ideas. The town is situated at the mouth of the Mzimvubu River, which flows through an impressive gorge flanked by two peaks, the "Gates of St. John." The peaks were called Mount Theysiger and Mount Sullivan, named after the two officers who first raised the British flag there in 1878. I walked down to the nearby beach to catch the ferry across the river. The 'ferry' was actually a small rowing boat and the pilot brought me across for three rand. After arriving on the opposite shore, I searched for a trail up Mount Sullivan but, for the life of me, I couldn't see any clearly defined path and feared none might exist. Still, I wasn't going to let that stop me so I ploughed ahead into the dense vegetation.

For the next forty minutes, I struggled through what I can only describe as the closest thing to jungle I have experienced. I had to force bushes out of my way, as thorny shrubs dragged at my pants. It was so humid, my shirt was soon drenched in sweat. Many times, I stopped and thought about turning back but, as they say, to go back would have been as hard as to go onward. I forged on, each time expecting to see the summit ahead some and, each time, being disappointed. Mercifully, the climb ended when I reached a clearing at the top and my efforts were rewarded with fine views of the town and the beach below.

It was then I saw others ambling towards me along a fine walking trail. How I missed it, I still don't know but I was relieved it existed. I returned via the walking trail and crossed the river on a competing ferry navigated by a ten-year-old boy.

With a bit of time on my hands, I relaxed in the town park and watched some local kids playing soccer. Men walked by hand-in-hand, laughing and joking like old friends. Holding hands is a common practice among friends in Xhosa culture. A young man joined me on the bench and introduced himself as Alex, the coach of the under-ten soccer team I had been watching.

"Do you know anywhere to get a beer?" I asked.

"Yes, Needles Hotel is nearby and is very good. I'll show you."

He jumped off the bench and grabbed my hand. I was caught off guard by this, but thought *when in Rome...* Hand-in-hand, we made our way towards the hotel. Needles had seen better days and the bar was dark and smelled of stale beer. I ordered two Castles and sat at the bar with Alex. A customer who fancied himself as a bit of a pool shark, challenged me to a game. He couldn't have been that good as I beat him easily. He stormed out of the bar, throwing the cue on the table in anger. Soon after, friends of Alex walked in and joined us. A drunk soon latched onto me, wanting to tell me about his misery-filled life. I tried to be polite, although it was difficult. Alex taught me to say, "I love you" in Xhosa – "Ndiya kuthanda". A few girls at a nearby table tittered at my efforts and I really wanted to test my new phrase on them. I thought better of it, however, as I was afraid of the reaction it might provoke from any boyfriends.

After saying goodbye to Alex and the patrons of the Needles Hotel bar, I walked merrily back toward the hostel. I liked what I had seen of Port St. Johns. It had a certain ramshackle charm lacking in other towns I visited. At one point, I stopped on the footpath and listened. Songs drifted up from a distant valley as pinpricks of lights dotted the blackness of Mount Theysiger like fireflies. The music of Africa filled the warm night air and I breathed it in. This was a moment to savour. I craned my neck to the sparkling night sky, enjoying the sound of happy people singing in their distant homes, competing with the chorus of squeaking crickets. It was the unmistakable onset of pondo fever, a welcome ailment causing travellers to fall in love with an area and making departure extremely difficult. For the first time in my journey, I really felt I was in Africa.

Walk the Wild Side

"But I have discovered the secret that after climbing a great hill, one only finds that there are many more hills to climb. I have taken a moment here to rest, to steal a view of the glorious vista that surrounds me, to look back on the distance I have come." — *Nelson Mandela, Long Walk to Freedom*

After packing our supplies, Allen and I left Port St. Johns and set off towards the Wild Coast. The 156-mile Transkei Hiking Trail goes from Port St. Johns to Coffee Bay and takes five days, but we opted instead to go as far as Mpande, a two-day trek. There would be no stores along the route so we had to carry all our food, water and clothing. To lighten the load, we left all non-essential gear at the hostel, intending to return for it after the hike was finished.

The hostel owner kindly dropped us to the official start of the trail, the Silaka Nature Reserve. I commented on the lovely beach near the town as we sped by in his Landcruiser.

"That's Second Beach, one of the best along the whole Wild Coast," he said, "Also the most dangerous."

"Powerful currents?" asked Allen.

"No, sharks," he replied. "Nearly every shark attack here has been fatal. Bull sharks patrol the area and are very aggressive." Suddenly, the picture-perfect beach with its enticing waves didn't seem so welcoming.

At the park entrance, we paid a small hiking permit at the ranger station and started on our way. Along the gentle trail, wildebeests grazed and vervet monkeys frolicked. The reserve is small, just over 1,000 acres, but rich in lush forests, flowers and bird-life, and we had it practically to ourselves. It was warm and humid, and before long, a steady stream of sweat trickled from my forehead onto the dusty ground. We emerged on a high vantage point, where we surveyed the reserve and beaches in the distance.

Allen kept the locals we met entertained with his impressions of an Italian tourist, full of hand expressions. He also raised his arms in triumph, shouting "Bafana, Bafana," the loving term for the South African soccer team who were playing in the World Cup. That always earned him a big cheer.

Once we left the reserve, we were into real hiking country. The marked trails disappeared, replaced with faint tracks that seemed to lead in different directions. We decided to keep the ocean to our left and forge ahead. Waves pummelled the rocky shore far below and I could see how the Wild Coast earned its name. Many ships met their doom along this treacherous coastline. The first few hours of the trek were tough, with rocky paths and undulating hills to cross, passing only grazing cattle and a few herders.

After five hours or so, I thought I saw a hotel in the distance. It could easily have been a mirage, as I hadn't expected to see such a place on our route. As we came closer, we realised it was a holiday resort. With a spring in our step, we quickened our pace towards what was sure to be salvation. Images of showers, three-course dinners and cold beers danced in my head, as we dragged our tired and sunburnt bodies towards the lovely Lagoon Lodge.

We must have cut some sight as we stumbled into the swanky reception. While the other guests ambled about in pressed shorts and spotless shirts, we presented ourselves with dust-caked legs, dirty t-shirts and sweat-streaked faces. I inquired if we could have a room, but was told the cheapest one available was 1,500 rand. Ashen faced at the price, I tried to use my Irish charm to plead with the old dear at reception for a generous discount, but my cajoling didn't fool her. There was to be no luxurious rest at this resort.

"This is not what we came on this hike for anyway Johnny," Allen said, as we left the resort. "Sure, this place is the same price as an average hotel in the States, but that's not what we came to see." Throwing an arm around my shoulder, he pointed at the hills to the north. "Adventure, excitement and a very basic hut awaits us over those hills," he laughed. Turning our backs on the exclusive resort, we plodded onwards.

We caught the nearby ferry across the Umngazi River before trudging over the energy-sapping sand dunes on the other side. The rest of the trail seemed to be a jumble of grassy hills where the odd cow grazed contentedly, oblivious to our passing. Thatched rondavels dotted the countryside and the waves of the Indian Ocean crashed against the jagged shore far below.

It was easy to get lost in such natural beauty and that is exactly what we did. We couldn't figure out where we were on the map, even though our huts were supposed to be nearby. Hikers can stay in designated huts along the route and this is what we were looking for. An hour before nightfall and we were still searching for our accommodation. We scrambled across hills and sand dunes, getting more lost with each turn we made.

I was exhausted at this stage and frequently sank to my knees on the grassy hillside, turning my face towards heaven before shouting, "Why do you mock me Lord?" much to Allen's amusement.

We slogged along for another forty minutes before coming to yet another crossing at the Mngazana River. We stopped some locals to enquire about the overnight huts and they pointed over the hill on the opposite side of the river. An entrepreneuring young kid, no more than seven-years-old, charged us five rand each to bring us across in his small boat.

On the other side of the hill, we found the small village of Madakeni. Chickens and ducks scattered at our approach as curious faces peeked from smoky huts. With the help of a young boy, we at last found our hut, one of a cluster on a gentle sloping field surrounded by palm fronds. The ocean lapped the rocky shore mere meters from the hut.

Trek huts on the Wild Coast

We were dismayed to find the hut locked, but a ranger soon appeared to let us into our blessed abode. The huts were government-owned and provided specifically for hikers on the Transkei Trail. The accommodation was basic, comprising of two bare bunks, a wooden table and a blue barrel of purified water. After unpacking, we hungrily devoured a delicious meal of peanut butter and spam sandwiches.

"You smell that?" Allen asked, sniffing the air.

"I sure do. It smells delicious," I replied.

The sweet aroma of barbeque wafted into our hut, enticing us to investigate. From our doorway, we saw two guys cooking over an open fire at a nearby hut. I convinced Allen it would be rude not to call over and say hello. The cooks were South African and were barbequing freshly-caught crayfish, marinated with spices and sauce. We made small talk while staring at the delectable food, hoping to be invited to share their feast. When no offer was forthcoming, we instead swiped a few bottles of Sprite and retreated back to our hut for another course of peanut butter and spam sandwiches.

With nothing to do for the rest of the evening, we relaxed and talked. I produced a bottle of vodka from my bag and used the last of the Sprite as a mixer. We didn't even have cups to drink from so I fashioned two by cutting an empty Sprite bottle in half, using each end as a cup. Once the Sprite was gone, the only mixer left was the purified water. Vodka and purified water is no martini but, after a few toasts, the taste receded and the conversation flowed.

I produced a book of poetry called *Moloney Up and At It* by the Irish bard, Brendan Kennelly. I encourage everybody to go and buy it as soon as you can – after buying all my other books first, of course. Anyway, I read a few poems as we drank. Kennelly's poetry is earthy and full of sex. Allen liked them right away, so much so that I offered him the book as a gift.

"One more poem before you hand over your treasure," demanded Allen, sloshing his vodka cocktail.

I stood in the middle of the earthen floor,

illuminated by Allen's torch and the flickering light of a candle. With the sound of the Indian Ocean lapping at the nearby shore, I recited my favourite Kennelly poem, *The Resurrection of Kate Finucane.* Despite having the very forgiving audience of one vodka-filled Yank, I felt I was performing at Carnegie Hall. Here I was, reciting Irish poetry to a half-drunk American in a thatched hut on the remote coast of South Africa.

Travel can lead you to some funny places.

My head was still groggy as we set off the following morning following a breakfast of — you guessed it — peanut butter and spam sandwiches. I paid for the late night party, my legs burning with pain as I struggled up more grassy hills. The hillside facing the ocean was weather-blasted and bare, while the more sheltered, southern side had grass for grazing cattle.

We passed through some small villages, where Allen took photos of the local people with his digital camera. Some of the children ran away frightened, while others approached cautiously as he offered to show them their pictures on the camera screen. We arrived at a nice beach and the trail seemed to follow it, judging from the footprints of other walkers in the muddy sand. Long-horned cattle lounged nearby, looking relaxed as they chewed the cud. The area was rich in cow dung so they must have been there a while. The gentle waves offered a refreshing swim to my sweat-soaked body, but the thought of bull sharks lurking offshore convinced me to stay on land.

When we came to the Mpande River, we scanned the area for any sign of a ferry crossing. There didn't seem to be any and we wondered if we had taken another wrong turn. We watched trekkers on the opposite side take their boots off and wade into the water. The river mouth turned out to be shallow and we were delighted to follow their lead, the cold water a tonic for my tired feet. After conquering another grassy hill, we arrived at Mpande and soon located the legendry Kraal Backpacker.

Kraal Backpacker

The Kraal was like a mini-fortress with commanding views over the ocean and the lovely Sinangwana Beach. The welcoming bar, decorated with driftwood, flotsam and shells, had the feel of a hippie paradise. Many people, stricken with pondo fever, lazed in hammocks and watched the world go by. There was no electricity, just candles and oil lamps to shed light.

After two days without washing, I was dying for a shower. I was a bit disappointed to learn I had to heat the water myself using wood as fuel. *Another adventure*, I thought. After an hour trying to heat enough water, I could wait no longer. It was enough for a short, warm shower but well worth the effort.

Refreshed, I wandered into the dining room. A large, wooden box filled with marijuana sat in the middle of the dining table.

"Durban gold, the best there is," boasted Dillon, owner of the Kraal. "Help yourself, but don't stuff it into your pockets or backpack. Use only what you need."

Dillon had sun-bleached hair and wore a necklace of seashells. I also noticed his eyes were different colours, one brown and one blue.

"Are you joining us for dinner? Don't miss it, it's a real treat tonight," Dillon promised and I readily accepted.

While waiting, I read a bit by candlelight, something I hadn't done in years. I then joined Allen and the other residents around the dining table. When the food arrived, I was pleasantly surprised. Succulent barbequed shrimp and pieces of baked salmon accompanied strips of steak and fresh Xhosa bread. I hadn't expected anything as delicious and gorged myself like a man who had eaten nothing but peanut butter and spam sandwiches for two days.

The following morning, I finally succumbed to a bout of pondo fever and lounged about the Kraal. It was a Thursday, the heavily anticipated night Dillon made space cakes for everyone.

Later that evening, I seated myself at the dining table again in anticipation of another great meal and wasn't disappointed. Afterwards, Dillon went round to each of us with a plate of drug-laced biscuits.

"Only take one each and remember, I'm not the devil," he smiled devilishly. I took one and ate it, waiting for something to happen. When I felt no effects, I ate another but still nothing. I began to think I was one of those people who are impervious to the effects of drugs when it hit me. Holy God, it was as if I was in another world. One minute, I was talking to Allen about seals and the next thing, I was laughing uncontrollably, in utter stiches. By the end of the night, I could hardly move my legs and Allen was no better. We had to be helped to our beds by Sarah, a kindly traveller who hadn't ingested any evil space cakes.

When we reached a short, wooden bridge that led to our room, I refused to go any further. What was previously an innocent bridge became a wildly swinging death trap over a bottomless chasm. No matter what, I could not be enticed to cross the bridge and Allen was in the same situation. With saintly patience, Sarah finally coaxed us across, leading us by the hands like scared, little children.

The next morning, after swearing off space cakes for a while at least, I spotted a few spear-guns behind the reception desk. I asked Dillon if we could borrow them for the day.

"You can have flippers and masks as well, but be bloody careful with this stuff," he warned us before handing over the gear. He told us about a small sea inlet not far from the Kraal, ideal for spear-fishing.

Spear-fishing was much more difficult than I imagined. Even when I had a big fish directly in my sights and only a few feet away, the spear failed to find its mark. It was also dangerous, as the strong currents nearly swept me out into the ocean a few times. After a lot of effort, I finally managed to spear a small specimen while Allen bagged two fat fish.

Trouble awaited us back at the Kraal, however, when we handed back the gear and thanked Dillon.

"Where is the other mask?" he asked. I realised I had left it on some rocks near the inlet. I returned to the spot but the mask was gone. I didn't know if it had been stolen or been washed out to sea. Dillon was not happy with the news.

"That mask was one of the most expensive pieces of equipment I have," he raged. He demanded we each pay about 300 rand for the mask unless it was returned. I didn't believe his evaluation at first, thinking he was trying to rip us off. That was until he produced a glossy diving catalogue and pointed out the same mask, confirming his estimate. Dillon also rounded up the local kids, warning them he would not buy crayfish from their communities until the mask was returned. His brown and blue eyes glowed red, as he raged at them in fluent Xhosa.

"There's a guy who could use a space cake right now," whispered Allen, nearly making me laugh and risk instant execution.

The mask had not appeared by the time we were ready to leave the Kraal, so we negotiated with Dillon and agreed to pay 200 rand each. I talked with Allen about hiking further along the Wild Coast, but decided we had enough. We hitched a ride from the Kraal to Port St. Johns on the back of a truck. We had different places to see, so this was where we parted company, for the time being at least.

Such is the way of a solo traveller. You meet people like Allen, share your life, your beers, your space cakes and your poetry. For a while, our lives shared the same trail and when it came time to go our separate ways, it was as friends.

6 PEOPLE OF GOD

Ever since arriving in South Africa, I had been looking out for a chance to volunteer and give my time to a worthy cause. While I was lucky enough to travel and see the world, it was a world where many lived in dire poverty. I didn't want to pass through South Africa without giving back a small token of my gratitude. A chance meeting offered me that very opportunity.

During my time in Durban, I stayed at the pleasant Hippo Hide in a residential area of the city. It was there I met a group of young, fresh-faced people with unmistakable Northern Ireland accents. I asked if they were backpacking around the country.

"No, we're here to volunteer at a centre for children orphaned by AIDS," said Naomi. "We're going to spend three months there."

This piqued my interest and I asked her to tell me more. "It's called God's Golden Acre, a place where we can comfort those children afflicted by AIDS." She looked at me and almost read my thoughts. "Why don't you come and volunteer yourself? They're always looking for more help."

I smiled and said I would definitely think about it.

In the meantime, it was another sunny day in Durban and I wanted to see the famous beaches of the city. As I waited for my taxi outside the hostel, streams of runners jogged by. I asked a departing guest what was going on.

"It's a public holiday today. These crazy guys are taking part in the Comrades Race, a 90-kilometre ultra-marathon from Durban to Pietermaritzburg. And in this heat," he exclaimed, pointing at the searing midday sun.

As I discovered later, the race originally commemorated the South African soldiers killed during WWI. Now, it is the ultimate endurance test for lovers of pain and suffering.

My taxi arrived to bring me to the waterfront. During the journey, I asked the coloured driver if things had changed since the new government took over. His hands tightened on the steering wheel.

"This government is no good, too corrupt," he exclaimed, little bits of spittle flying onto the dashboard, punctuating his fury. "Nothing has changed since the whites left power. I say to you honestly," he continued, turning to face me in the back seat while driving along a busy road, "I would welcome the old system back again. Things were better then. There was no crime and everyone had a job. Not like now, with blacks committing crime everywhere."

I would hear the same racist rant from others on my journey. Again, I felt like saying something but didn't. What did I know of this man's experiences? What did I know about life in South Africa? Others I met would complain that progress was too slow in health, security and education. Government ministers drove big cars while common people lived in shacks. It was a predictable combination of no jobs for young people, coupled with rising crime.

The driver dropped me at the Golden Mile, a stretch of beach near downtown Durban. I wasn't planning on swimming, just enjoying the sea air. I strolled along the lovely promenade in the company of ordinary Durbanites. Old ladies sporting large sunglasses walked their small dogs, fashionably dressed mothers pushed their designer prams, sweat-soaked joggers huffed by, groups of cyclists weaved around pedestrians while many others, like myself, just walked. Colourful sun umbrellas and bronzed bodies dotted the beach as swimmers walked past a line of surfboards impaled in the white sand. A gentle sea breeze offered welcome relief from the heat of the day.

I stopped to stare at a passing rickshaw driver. He wore a gigantic headdress of multi-coloured feathers that seemed impossible to support by a single neck. It towered above him and must have been punishing to wear, no matter how spectacular it looked. Further along the promenade, heavily muscled men in ripped t-shirts chatted up buxom blondes outside one of the many bars that lined the strip.

I stopped at 'Joe Kool's' for a beer and some mediocre food. The place was full of surfers with sandy hair, knee-length shorts and faded t-shirts. They slouched in booths, talking about the next big wave in that laid-back way of surfers.

After leaving the bar, I wandered toward the city centre, even though I had been warned not to do so at the hostel. It amazed me how suddenly the energy changed going from one street to another. One minute, I was walking along without a care in the world and a little while later, I seriously thought about doubling back. I felt that everyone loitering on street corners was staring at me, every shout directed toward me. Despite that, the allure of the Indian Market on Victoria Street was too great to resist.

Durban has a large Indian population that came to the area as indentured workers from the 1860s onwards, mainly to toil on the sugarcane plantations. Without doubt, the most famous of those migrants was Mahatma Gandhi. Gandhi's most pivotal moment in the country came during a train journey from Durban to Pretoria. A white passenger complained about having to share his carriage with a 'coolie', even though Gandhi had a first-class ticket. A train official asked Gandhi to move to the third-class carriage but he refused. Along with his luggage, he was thrown off the train at Pietermaritzburg, where he spent the night in the station waiting room. "It was winter," Gandhi wrote in his autobiography, "and the cold was extremely bitter. My over-coat was in my luggage, but I did not dare to ask for it lest I should be insulted again, so I sat and shivered." He later said it was one of the most decisive events in his life and one which propelled him to fight for Indian rights in South Africa and later, for Indian independence.

I wondered what might have happened if the white passenger had not complained, leaving Gandhi to reach Pretoria unhindered. *Would he have gone on to be the inspirational figure he was?* By such quirks of fate, great men are born.

One of the many contributions Indians made to Durban was the excellent market, housed in a building modelled on a Maharajah's palace. Once I stepped inside, I was magically transported to India. Women wrapped in bright yellow saris sat on plastic stools before shops draped with riotously coloured garlands. Indian and African music

played in the background while women in blue
Muslim headdress sat outside fish stalls. Enticing
smells of curry and cardamom coaxed me from
shop to shop. Sweating spice vendors displayed
colourful hills of bright red curry powder alongside
luminous green fish-spice (No, I don't know what
that is either). The spices had amusing names such
as *Mother-in-law Hellfire*, *Honeymooners Special* and,
the intriguing named, *Mother-in-law Exterminator*. I
wandered through the incense-infused air with the
constant chatter of bargaining around me. I left the
market wishing that my impending visit to India
could come sooner.

God's Golden Acre

Durban had plenty of attractions to keep me
longer, but the chance to volunteer was too good to
miss. I called the folks at God's Golden Acre (GGA)
and asked if I could stay for a while. They gladly
agreed and arranged to collect me outside a coffee
shop called Jug and Bean. There, I was introduced
to the other volunteers before we set off. I asked the
lovely Australian, Simone, more about what GGA
does.

"We take in children who have lost parents to
AIDS and don't have any surviving family to care
for them. We do this with the blessing of the local
villages in the valley. Some of the children also
have AIDS and don't have long to live."

"There are nearly 900,000 AIDS orphans in KwaZulu-Natal alone," said the South African driver, Mornè, without taking his eyes off the road. "It's almost too big to think about."

KwaZulu-Natal is the epicentre of South Africa's AIDS epidemic. An estimated one third of the province's 9.9 million inhabitants are HIV-positive.

After a two-hour journey, we arrived at God's Golden Acre. It was a former leisure complex donated to GGA for the benefit of the children. A number of buildings served as volunteer accommodation while others housed the children. I was told I would be staying with Gunther, a German who had been working at the centre for the past year. He welcomed me to his spartan, two-bedroom concrete hut, offering me the spare room.

"I helped build this hut after I first arrived but, as you see, it still needs work," he said, rubbing his hand along the rough, unplastered walls. I thanked him for letting me stay and unpacked my things. Afterwards, I joined him in the small kitchen where he was rolling a joint.

"You want one?" he asked, offering me the cigarette he had just rolled. I accepted and we both enjoyed a smoke in the chilly room. I was glad I packed my sleeping bag, as the hut was poorly insulated and a cold draught blew under the front door. I hadn't expected to see my freezing breath during my time in South Africa.

I rose early the following day, full of the spirit of charity and ready to help people, whether they bloody liked it or not. I imagined what I would achieve by the end of that week. I would bring laughter and new energy to the place. Children that previously spoke to nobody would be chatting to me non-stop. Their faces would brighten at my approach, the lame would walk and the blind see. Okay, not really, but you see the mood I was in that morning. I bumped into Simone on the way to the office.

"Anything you'd like me to help you with?" I asked, giving her the flirtiest smile I could muster.

"Well, I have just the job for you John," she said, with a twinkle in her eye. She led me to a large corrugated iron building, which housed all clothing donations the centre received. Wooden shelves ran the length of the building and each one overflowed with jumbled clothes right up to the roof. It seemed the very walls of the building were constructed of used clothing.

Simone then assumed a business-like tone.

"Now, we need to sort all these clothes for boys and girls. First, we'll make one heap for boy's trousers, ages 0-2, one for boy's tops, aged 0-2 and likewise for girls. Then, group boy's tops and trousers, ages 2-4..."

My mind trailed away as I realised my charitable contribution to the people of South

Africa would be sorting a mountain of clothing. Not exactly what I originally had in mind. I couldn't very well complain so I got stuck in. The tedious task was made all the easier by having such good company in Simone. She had a ready smile and infectious laugh I found very attractive. After four hours, I reached the boy's tops, ages 6-10. Despite Simone's company, I couldn't face another image of Mickey Mouse so I gave up for the day, returning to the hut for a nap.

Later that evening, Gunther brought me to a South African barbeque, or *braai*, hosted by George. George was a South African who had worked at the centre for a number of years. Other volunteers chatted around the braai fire, which had been fashioned by cutting a steel oil-drum in half. Sausages, steaks and burgers sizzled over the flames, as everyone unwound after the day with food and beer.

George was responsible for construction projects at the centre. I told him about my day sorting children's clothes and he sympathised, inviting me to help him with a building project the following day. I readily accepted.

While waiting for my burger to cook, I asked people why there was such a problem with AIDS in the area.

"Education for one thing," said a guy holding a beer in one hand and a hotdog in the other. "Did you know in 1999, the health department inadvertently stapled holes in condoms while attempting to attach user instruction pamphlets?" I shook my head incredulously.

"It's true. When the health department is this ignorant about how to use condoms, you're in real trouble."

I was kept awake that night by Gunther having sex. When I pressed him for details the following morning, he wouldn't say who the lucky girl was.

"No, no, I cannot tell you," he smiled, pushing his blonde hair back from his face before taking another drag of his joint.

Feeling grumpy and unrested, I headed over to the site where George was busy at work. He was building a concrete rondavel and quickly put me to work shovelling sand and mixing concrete. It felt great to be doing some outdoor work instead of sorting clothes. I thought about my previous job, sitting behind a desk at a financial company in Boston, attending mind-numbing meetings and bashing away at a keyboard. There is something refreshing and rewarding about manual labour that an office environment could never match. You know you've earned your dinner after a day swinging the pick and using the spade.

George finished working after lunch, leaving me free for the evening. I bumped into Hugh, a volunteer working with the charity World Vision, a non-government organisation (NGO). He invited me to go with him to a local Zulu village.

"We're trying to establish a child-sponsorship program to raise funds for GGA," Hugh told me, as we drove towards the village. "Many NGOs have the same type of program. We collect child profiles and, hopefully, people will decide to sponsor them."

The village was a collection of mud huts with ragged kids running about. Hugh spoke to some parents and took notes. It was hard to imagine what the people thought, seeing a bunch of white foreigners come to their village and quiz them about their children. A young kid, no more than 7 years old, offered me a stick of sugarcane while I waited for Hugh. We sat on the bare earth together and enjoyed the sweet treat in silence.

Rural hut in KwaZulu-Natal

On the way back to the centre, I was lost in thought. I couldn't understand why these kids were dressed in rags when there was a warehouse bursting at the seams with clean, warm clothes only a few miles away.

"Not even sure myself," admitted Hugh. "I think GGA are holding off on the distribution of clothes until sponsorship programs have been set up."

I nodded my head but did not understand at all.

I stared out the window in silence for the remainder of the journey. I felt guilty. I was well off and white and they were poor and black. I asked myself, *was guilt the main reason I wanted to volunteer, to do something, anything?* Was I volunteering, not because I really wanted to help people, but to alleviate my guilt? I began to think my whole reason for being there was not charitable, but selfish.

Back to the centre, it was off to George's place for another braai. His home was the social centre of GGA and with good reason. George was laid back, well-liked and his door was always open. The smell of barbequing meat and the sound of laughter were never far from his place.

I was back at work on the building site the next day. The rondavel was quickly taking shape. Working hard, we completed the circular walls of the building by lunchtime. We put in a few more hours after lunch before knocking off for the day.

Later that evening, Mornè asked me to go with him and Hugh to pick up a volunteer at a local village. On the way, I noticed they both seemed tense. I asked Mornè why he needed me to accompany them.

"Carjacking is common in this area at night," he admitted. "It happened to me only last week. An armed gang stopped my bakkie (truck) and got in. One of them ordered me to show him how to drive. Can you believe it? The bastards didn't know how to drive. I just kept talking, telling them how to operate the gears and pedals. Once they got the hang of it, they ordered me out and drove off."

"Most times, they just kill the driver so he was

very lucky," Hugh said.

"They didn't get my bakkie though," laughed Mornè, "Those punks crashed it into a ditch a short way from where they left me out."

After hearing this, I felt as tense as they were. Every shadow the headlights picked out became a hijacker with a gun. It wasn't until we had safely collected the volunteer and returned to the centre that I could relax.

Later that evening, I returned to George's for beers. Everyone was in good form and enjoying the evening. Suddenly, there was a loud noise from outside.

"What was that?" asked Gunther, "Sounded like someone breaking into one of the huts."

George leapt to his feet and said something to Mornè in Afrikaans before grabbing some sticks and heading for the door. Their transformation was sudden and frightening. One minute, they were laughing and enjoying themselves, the next, they were ready to kill someone. For the first time in South Africa, I felt afraid. Nevertheless, I felt I had to follow them, just in case they needed help. Thankfully, the commotion was blamed on a stray dog knocking over a rubbish bin. Everyone relaxed and returned to the braai.

"I was robbed blind only three weeks ago," George told me on the way back. "They took my computer and music system. It cost me a lot of money."

Before returning to my hut that night, I asked George if I could borrow his cat. Spliff was a grey Tomcat, the size of a terrier and as mean as a Rottweiler. I hoped he might catch a rat I suspected was running about my bedroom at night.

The next morning, Spliff had gone, probably bolted back to George under the door. I wandered into the kitchen for breakfast only to see a strange black woman busy washing the dishes.

"If you need any clothes washed, you can give them to the cleaning lady and she'll have them back by end of day tomorrow," Gunther told me in between mouthfuls of breakfast cereal. I was amazed that, even as volunteers, we could afford a cleaner. At first, I was tempted to refuse, thinking it felt too much like exploitation to use another person because I was too lazy to wash my own clothes. However, I suspected she depended on people like me to earn a small income, so I gave her my clothes and thanked her profusely.

Later that evening, I was in a particularly volunteering mood and offered to help feed the children at suppertime. From overheard conversations around George's braai, this was the most challenging part of the day for volunteers and I wanted to see what the fuss was about. There was no going back once I opened the doors of the dining room.

The place looked like a prison during a riot. Kids stood on tables, flinging food across the room while half-naked children ran around in circles screaming. Simone and two other volunteers struggled to cope as the little devils paid no heed to any orders or cajoling.

On seeing the chaos, I attempted to quietly retreat through the door before Simone spotted me.

"John, thank God. Can you watch this crew for a minute while we pop out and get something?"

I nodded meekly and accepted my fate.

Simone and her friend bolted through the door, leaving me standing in the middle of the room with no idea about what to do next. Food flew everywhere, kids crawled on tables, and one little girl peed into a cup.

For the love of God, don't drink that.

One of the kids in particular seemed to rouse the others to greater heights of mayhem and really tested my patience.

"Now come on, stop throwing food everywhere will you?" I pleaded with him. He graced me with an angelic smile before grabbing a handful of spaghetti and flinging it over the head of the peeing girl.

After what felt like the longest hour in my life, Simone returned. I had never been so relieved to see her lovely face. Between us, we managed to get a few children into the bath. Once they were tucked up in bed, I read a story to two young boys. I was sure they had heard *Jack and the Beanstalk* a hundred times before, but never in an Irish accent. A few stories later, they fell asleep and I left the room quietly, breathing a huge sigh of relief.

How the hell does anyone deal with kids at all, I wondered?

Later at George's, I met Simone again and asked her about the children's background.

"Almost all of them have a sad story. Some are living with HIV and a few have died of AIDS during my time here," she admitted. "Many come from backgrounds where they have been physically and sexually abused, while others have been abandoned. Nearly all the kids here are affected by HIV in some way."

By way of thanks for their generosity, I invited all the volunteers to an Irish evening at George's hut. I picked up a load of meat and vegetables at the local store and prepared an Irish stew, using the biggest pot I could find. I think my mother would have been proud of my effort. The hearty stew was complimented with bottles of Castle Milk Stout, the South African attempt at Guinness.

Gunther was excited about the following day, as Germany was playing Brazil in the World Cup final. I helped him move his sofa to George's place, where it was used as an outdoor lounge to watch the game. Gunther generously laid out plenty of beers and snacks for the party. Unfortunately, Brazil beat Germany 2-0, deflating poor Gunther a little.

Everyone else was in high spirits, however, so we decided to make the most of it. George suggested we move the party to a scenic spot high above the valley. We put the braai in the back of his tractor-trailer and George began to pull away. In his haste, he forgot to secure the trailer to the tractor. The trailer soon came away from the tractor, leaving us all stranded as George drove off, oblivious to his laughing cargo.

Once properly connected, we arrived at a scenic spot on top of a small hill, overlooking the entire valley. We lifted the smoking braai onto the field and admired the view. The wind had picked up and the grass around the braai was bone-dry - a recipe for disaster. Someone knocked over the braai and within seconds, the whole area was engulfed in flames. The wind spread the fire with terrifying speed. Never have a bunch of people sobered up as quickly. I pulled off my sweater and started beating the flames in a desperate attempt to stop the fire's progress. Looking up, I saw a shirtless Gunther doing the same while shouting, "Save the centre, let everything else burn."

The fire was out of control and I stood back from the flames with my blackened sweater in hand, helplessly watching the raging fire spread across the surrounding countryside. I had images of standing before a judge, trying to explain how instead of assisting the underprivileged children of the area, I helped burn down their orphanage. That was how serious it was. After an hour, the fire around the centre burned itself out without causing any damage to the buildings. Everyone was exhausted, but relieved. I returned to George's in a much quieter mood than I had left it. My hand trembled as I downed a beer, watching a myriad of distant fires through the window.

The next morning, I climbed aboard the same bus that had brought me to God's Golden Acre. I thanked everyone for giving me the chance to spend some time at the centre. I had hoped that something might have happened with Simone but, like the grasslands around the centre, my chance went up in flames the previous night. However, I did give her a huge hug that lingered longer than was decent. Whatever about my own reasons for being there, Simone, Gunther, Hugh, George and Mornè were good people who genuinely wanted to help the children. The world could do with a lot more people like them.

7 ZULULAND

Shakaland

To this day, I have vivid memories of watching a television series about the great Zulu king, Shaka. Even though I was young at the time, certain gory scenes stayed with me, such as one episode where Shaka had his enemies impaled on sharpened poles. The image of their bodies writhing like beetles stayed with me for a long time. Throughout the series, Shaka sought advice from a ghostly witchdoctor, whose eyes glowed red with menace every time she spoke. I went to bed every night thankful I never had to encounter those terrifying and bloodthirsty Zulu warriors.

That was until I visited them at Shakaland.

According to my guidebook, "The slightly Disneyfied Shakaland offers a touristy blend of perma-grin performance and informative authenticity." For me, that was not how culture should be experienced and I vowed never to set foot on its soil. However, when my Swiss roommate, Maurice, offered me a lift there, I happily accepted. I was bored and my values were a little more flexible then.

"I am very interested in the history of Shaka," Maurice told me on the way. "They called him the black Napoleon because he conquered much of southern Africa."

"I heard he was a barbarian who killed thousands of innocent people," I replied.

"Yes, but he was also a great military genius. You will see when we get there," he said, shifting in his seat with excitement. I didn't have very high expectations of the place, but I couldn't help but admire Maurice's enthusiasm.

Upon arrival, we purchased tickets at the reception and joined other tourists as we waited for our guide. He arrived soon after and welcomed us to Zululand.

"I will be your guide during your stay at Zululand but first, it is a Zulu custom to ask the chief for permission to enter his village. If he agrees, your safety and comfort will be his responsibility while you are there."

We marched to the village entrance where our guide shouted a greeting in Zulu to the distant chief. He responded positively and our guide ushered us into the compound through a gate capped with giant buffalo horns.

Shakaland started as a film set for the television series *Shaka Zulu*, the same one that made such an impression on me as a child. Several authentic Zulu kraals were constructed for the series and all but one was burned for the final scene. Shaka's original capital, Bulawayo, lay a short distance from the current Shakaland. Not to be confused with the city in Zimbabwe with the same name, Bulawayo is loosely translated as 'Place of Slaughter'.

Shaka was born the illegitimate son of a Zulu chief around 1787. Shaka and his mother, Nandi, were cast out to live with another tribe, the Langeni. As a young man, he was weak, scrawny and ridiculed by other boys. They would later pay a terrible price for their teasing.

The chief invited us to enjoy all his village had to offer. He wore a leopard skin draped around his neck and chest, while bright feathers fluttered from his head. He also carried a spear and cowhide shield.

Our guide took a stick and drew an outline of the Zulu village in the dust. It consisted of two concentric circles. The beehive huts were situated inside the outer circle while the cattle, the wealth of any Zulu community, were kept inside the inner circle, known as the *kraal*.

Our guide showed us to the main hall, which was really an oversized beehive hut. Inside, war shields and cowhides decorated the walls. A group of performers dressed in traditional clothing waited as we took our seats. The women took to the floor, accompanied by singing and clapping from the assembled men behind them. They wore colourful mini-skirts, while strings of beads covered their otherwise delightfully bare breasts. Some danced with enthusiasm, while others looked bored and disinterested. The dance culminated in a series of head-high kicks, causing skirts and beads to fly into the air. They could have danced like that forever as far as I was concerned.

Maurice interrupted my happy reverie. "In Zulu culture, topless women are single. They dress more modestly once they get married," he whispered. I muttered a word of thanks before quickly returning to my cultural education.

The drumming tempo increased as the chief entered, flanked by bare-chested warriors carrying large cowhide shields. He took his place on the throne while the men readied themselves for their performance.

Their dance was full of energetic foot stomping and high kicks. They wore animal skins around their waists and lower legs. As the drumming got louder, they thrust their spears skywards while waving their cowhide shields around enthusiastically. Women clapped and whistled, adding to the energy and excitement.

"Those short stabbing spears were invented by Shaka," Maurice told me, referring to the weapons carried by the dancers. "Before, warriors threw spears at each other. Shaka saw how useless that was and instead created this weapon called the *assegai*. Warriors used it in close combat with very good effect," he said, jabbing his thumb into my ribs in demonstration.

A four-year-old boy clad in a tiny loincloth appeared towards the end of the show and drew the loudest cheer of the evening when he mimicked the dance of the adults, kicking his little legs into the air to laughter and applause.

After the performance, we stayed seated for a demonstration of traditional Zulu beer making. A container of beer was passed around for each of us to taste. Like the Xhosa beer I sampled at Coffee Bay, it looked like milk and tasted horrible.

We then left the hall and our guide brought us to a restaurant where we enjoyed a lovely meal. Maurice insisted on giving me a history lesson as we ate.

"When the Zulu King Dingiswayo was murdered in 1816, Shaka took the throne by impaling the rightful heir," Maurice said, spearing a piece of meat with his knife.

"Shaka seems to have been fond of impaling," I observed.

"Oh, he was," Maurice nodded. "One of the first things he did after becoming king was to take revenge on the unfortunate Langeni tribe. Those who had mocked him and his mother were taken before him and either clubbed or impaled to death."

"Is it true he once locked a woman in a hut with a starving hyena," I asked, remembering a scene from the television series.

"Not true, it was a jackal," he said, wiping his mouth with a napkin. "When his chief was murdered, Shaka took revenge by locking the assassin's mother in a small hut with starving jackals. It may have taken days before she fell asleep and the famished animals devoured her. This act of cruelty was strange because he loved his mother very much. When she died, he was overcome with grief and anger. He ordered no crops were to be planted that year and no milk to be used. Any woman who became pregnant was killed along with her husband. Cows were even slaughtered so that their calves would know what losing a mother felt like."

After lunch, our guide took us on a tour of the village. Women sat outside their huts making Zulu beadwork with hidden messages. The sequence of coloured beads could contain a message such as an expression of love. A woman wearing the traditional Zulu attire of a red, flat-topped hat and blue tunic sat on the ground under a sort of loom, weaving straw into mats. Basket weavers displayed their work, bound so tightly to be watertight. Potters shaped and baked their wares. The demonstration on hut construction showed how wooden frames were thatched with straw, while the floor was created by pounding a mixture of clay and cow dung.

We were then shown to the hut of the witchdoctor, the character that haunted my dreams as a child.

"There are two types of traditional healers in Zulu culture," our guide told us. "The *sangomas* and the *inyangas*. Sangomas are born with gifts of vision and fortune telling, while inyangas undergo training to become healers. The Zulu people revere the sangoma as a spiritual leader and healer. Ancestors are very important in Zulu culture and the sangoma is believed to be able to communicate with them."

Outside, women demonstrated how to carry heavy, clay pots full of water on their heads. Some women in our group were gently coerced into trying this for themselves. Even when empty, nobody managed to balance the jars on their heads for more than a few seconds. It showed the neck strength required to carry such heavy weights on a daily basis.

As we left the village, I asked Maurice how Shaka died.

"He died the way most Zulu kings did, murdered by members of his own family, this time by his half-brothers. How do you say, he lived by the sword and he died by the sword."

Before leaving, I popped into the gift shop to buy some souvenirs. Amongst the various items, I picked up an unusual wicker ball. I read the information panel on the back, informing me the device was a penis sheath, reputedly invented by Shaka himself. Known as the 'mad man's hut', it was designed to control the raging hormones of Shaka's married warriors while away from home.

I went with the tea towels instead.

Hluhluwe-Imfolozi Park

While Kruger National Park is the crown jewel of South Africa's wildlife reserves, the country is also blessed with a string of smaller, but no less exciting, places to view animals. The following day, I joined Maurice on a visit to the nearby Hluhluwe-Imfolozi Park.

On the way, we overtook a slow-moving truck, laden with sugarcane. Children jogged after the vehicle, gorging themselves on the long stalks of sweetness they pulled from the cargo. Smoke rose from a multitude of fires in every blackened sugarcane plantation we passed, as if a retreating army had scorched the countryside. The changing wind blew palls of smoke across the road, filling the car with the unmistakable smell of burnt sugar.

After the town of Ulundi, the road to Hluhluwe-Imfolozi deteriorated into a dirt track. We finally reached the park and paid a small fee at the ranger's booth. Once inside, we followed the road along a meandering river. The park was first proclaimed a protected area in 1895, making it the oldest game reserve in South Africa. Even before that, Shaka had declared the land as protected, an untypically compassionate move on his behalf. The park is roughly the size of Greater London with only a third accessible to tourists.

It wasn't long before I spotted my first wild animal in South Africa. A white rhino stood motionless about a hundred feet from our slowing car. With skin like a tank and armed with a deadly horn, it looked like the most dangerous animal in the world. At least it would have were it not for the little bird sauntering happily along its back, seeming to mock the great beast beneath it. Despite its name, the rhino is not white, coming instead from the Afrikaans word for wide, *wijd*, referring to the animal's wide lower lip.

A while later, our passing car startled a family of warthogs, sending them scurrying into the bush with their tails pointing comically into the air. Despite their menacing tusks and ugly looks, I couldn't help but laugh at the way they ran. A group of three zebras, adorned with magnificent black and white stripes, took little notice while I photographed them. They raised their heads once to ensure we posed no threat before returning to their foraging. Impala seemed to be everywhere, our approach sending herds of them running for their lives. We also spotted some springbok, the symbol of the South African rugby team.

The leaflet I picked up at the park entrance warned us to look out for fresh elephant dung, as it was a sign the animal may be in the vicinity. As we drove around a bend, I pointed at a little hill of steaming dung on the road and wondered aloud if an elephant was nearby. As if on cue, something caught the corner of my eye and I turned to see a gigantic, grey elephant emerging from the bushes on our right. I took a sharp intake of breath and jabbed my finger wordlessly, fearing any sound might spook the great beast into an attack.

Maurice killed the engine and we just sat there, awestruck by this close encounter with a goliath of nature. I never realised just how big elephants were until I saw one up close. I had watched YouTube videos of them flipping cars and charging at tourists with their ears outstretched — a sight I hope I'll never see. The elephant paused for a few seconds in front of the car before continuing its leisurely journey across the dusty road. I watched as the deeply wrinkled giant disappeared into the bush before whooping with joy.

KwaZulu-Natal had given me a taste of its bloody history, but also its incredible animal diversity. I bade farewell to Maurice at Eshowe and ventured north to see the province's other famous park. It was time to leave the land for a while.

8 SODWANA BAY

'The Sea, once it casts its spell, holds one in its net of wonder forever' – Jacques Cousteau

St. Lucia

My main reason for coming to the small town of St. Lucia was to see the iSimangaliso Wetland Park. Previously known as Greater St. Lucia Wetland Park, the area is a little strip of paradise hugging the northeast coast of South Africa. *Isimangaliso* is a Zulu word meaning 'miracle' and the park promises the miracle of nature, both on land and sea. The biodiversity of the reserve is the main attraction. Rich coral reefs offshore boast impressive marine-life such as whales, dolphins, and loggerhead turtles, while the wetlands are home to elephants, leopards, rhinos, and buffalos.

I checked into Bib's Hostel on the banks of St. Lucia estuary and got talking to the owner, Sean. "Fancy seeing some hippos?" he asked. I nodded and, along with a few other backpackers, Sean ushered us into a small boat tied up just below the hostel. Within minutes, we were trailing across the estuary towards the setting sun, nervously watching crocodiles slide into the water from muddy embankments. Sean took us close to a group of hippos wallowing in the water. The loveable hippo would be the last on anybody's list of the most dangerous animals in Africa. With its friendly face and rotund, huggable body, it seems as harmless as its Disney image. However, the reality is much different.

"One of the most dangerous animals in Africa," Sean said in a whisper. "Hippos kill more people every year than lions, sharks or snakes. Their teeth are like elephant ivory and can cut a person in two." He let us digest this information before adding, "Still, more people are killed every year by champagne corks so it's still a small number."

I asked Sean if hippos had killed any locals.

"Hippos regularly roam the streets of the town," he said. "After all, St. Lucia is within the park bounds. However, the only deaths in recent years occurred when a hippo was shooed off a woman's lawn and onto the road, where a car hit it and killed the passengers."

The water suddenly boiled around the hippos.

"Females shitting on the males," Sean informed us casually. "It's the way they show loyalty to their mates."

"Bloody women, same everywhere," joked one brave soul, quickly followed by a hard thump to his shoulder by his unimpressed girlfriend.

"Hippos spend most of their time in the water," Sean continued, "because their legs aren't strong enough to carry their weight on land for long. Despite their appearance, they can outrun most humans." He stopped as the water erupted with another female displaying her loyalty.

"Hippos can also walk underwater but need to surface for air every 3 to 5 minutes. They can do this automatically while asleep, rising to the surface and breathing without waking."

Someone on the boat asked about a hippo called Huberta. Sean turned the boat for home and told us the story behind this remarkable creature.

Huberta the Hippo

In November of 1928, a solitary female hippo left St. Lucia and embarked on a three-year trek southward. Surprisingly, she did not try to avoid people and passed through many busy towns and cities. Thousands followed Huberta's progress and she became famous, not only in South Africa, but in

Britain and the United States as well.

Huberta evaded many attempts to capture her and move her to a zoo. She even amused holidaymakers on one of Durban's beaches, swimming in the sea and sauntering on the beach. She also trampled over the elite Beachwood Golf Course and arrived uninvited to an exclusive party at the Durban Country Club, ambling along the veranda as partygoers danced.

In March of 1931, Huberta reached East London, having travelled over 1,600 kilometres. Both the Zulu and Xhosa alike revered Huberta as a great spirit. She was declared royal game, which should have afforded her protection from hunters. Alas, it was not to be. While wallowing in a nearby river a month later, she was shot and killed by three hunters.

There was a national outcry and the police tracked down her killers. They pleaded ignorance about her identity, only being fined £25 each for destroying royal game. That was not the end of the story, however. Despite her death, Huberta's allure continued. Her body was recovered and sent to a taxidermist in London. On her return to South Africa in 1932, over 20,000 people flocked to see Huberta on display at the Durban Museum. Today, her preserved body is on display in King William's Town, in the Eastern Cape.

Sodwana Bay

Ever since I can remember, the underwater world has held a deep fascination for me. When a place opened up on a scuba dive course in Sodwana Bay, I jumped at the opportunity.

Sodwana Bay is located within the iSimangaliso Wetland Park and is an ideal location for diving because of its pristine waters and proximity to numerous reefs. Each reef is named after the distance from the launch point, providing beginner, intermediate, or expert level dives.

I left St. Lucia on a local minibus and, after numerous stops to pick up and drop off passengers, arrived at Sodwana Bay. After paying a long list of registration fees, I was shown to my accommodation. The large, green tent was roomy enough to stand in and ideal for my needs.

Returning to my tent after a shower the following morning, I chased away two monkeys messing with the tent flap. After breakfast, I went to reception to collect materials for the scuba course and bumped into Mick, an Australian traveller I had met in Durban. We joined the other diving students at the theory class led by Fiona, our lovely dive instructor. I told her about the attempted break-in by monkeys and she smiled.

"That happens a lot," she said. "They were probably trying to unzip the flap and get into your tent."

"Monkeys aren't smart enough to do that, are they?" I asked.

"Monkeys in Sodwana Bay have become very used to people and can be very determined. A band of monkeys once mugged a local woman on her way home with a bag of fruit, forcing her to abandon her shopping and run."

I spent that evening in my tent studying for a written exam the following morning.

The exam was straightforward and everyone passed. Afterwards, Fiona led us to the nearby swimming pool. The first thing we had to do was swim twenty laps of the pool and then tread water for ten minutes, which was very tiring. We also practiced breathing underwater with a scuba mask and air regulator. Another task was sharing an air regulator to someone without air, a skill I sincerely hoped I would never need to use. Meanwhile, others were still doing laps above me.

I had nearly completed my final task when someone's underwear appeared in front of my mask on its way to the bottom of the pool. I exploded laughing and nearly choked on a few mouthfuls of water.

I was excited and looking forward to the next few days.

At breakfast the following morning, I encountered the legendary One-Eyed Jack. I left my food on an outdoors table to enjoy the morning sunshine and returned to the kitchen to get a coffee. Returning to my table, I discovered my toast had disappeared. The couple seated next to me were bent over laughing, pointing up at a nearby tree. There sat a verdant monkey, munching on my toast and wiping strawberry jam off his mouth with his little hairy hands. *There's a first time for everything*, I thought, as I returned for another slice.

"You probably won't believe me," I told the cook, "but a monkey just stole my toast and I'll need another."

"Oh, that'll be One-Eyed Jack so," said the cook, sliding a fresh slice of toast onto my plate. "He's a notorious thief. The roof is littered with salt and pepper shakers he stole from tables over the years. The previous cook tried to kill him with a catapult, but only succeeded in knocking out one of his eyes."

After hearing that story, I decided Jack deserved the toast more than I did.

Our first open water dive was scheduled for the following morning and I journeyed to the beach in a good mood, looking forward to seeing the wonders of the ocean. After all, there was a possibility I might encounter a dinosaur of the seas. In 1938, a strange fish caught off the coast of East London was identified as a coelacanth, a 200 million year old species thought to have been extinct over 50 million years ago. In 2000, another was caught near Sodwana Bay. Those waters held life thought to be extinct millions of years ago.

This was not just your everyday dive.

Conditions didn't look promising, however. Large waves pounded the shore as a strong wind whipped in from the sea. I expected the crew to postpone the dive but, to my surprise, it proceeded as planned.

We nervously clambered aboard a large inflatable boat equipped with an outboard motor and set off into the fierce seas. From the beginning, I had a bad feeling about the day. I sat on the gunwale of the boat, as it rose and fell through waves nearly four meters high. A girl sitting opposite me cupped her mouth, sick spewing through her fingers. Every time the boat hit a wave, we were pitched into the air before being plunged back into the sea, dousing everyone with seawater. After the third such battering, the girl opposite me started to sob quietly.

We reached the dive spot and, after a struggle, the crew managed to secure the boat to a buoy. I got into my scuba gear with a mixture of fear and anxiety. The fierce conditions did not look suitable for experienced divers, never mind a boatful of novices, but I assumed the crew knew what they were doing. I struggled to generate enough spit to coat the inside of my mask. This prevented my mask from fogging up underwater. I checked my gear and tested my air regulator. Mick was my 'dive buddy', the person responsible for double-checking that my diving equipment was in working order before getting in the water. Once I reciprocated, we were ready.

The dive master instructed us to sit on the edge of the boat with our backs to the sea. When instructed, I placed the air regulator in my mouth, leaned backwards and tumbled into the water. Bubbles burst around me until my buoyancy control device (BCD), a fancy word for an air-filled vest, pulled me upright. I touched the top of my head to signal I was okay before swimming towards the wave-lashed buoy. I released air from my BCD and slowly sank beneath the waves.

Breathing underwater is a strange sensation and takes some getting used to. My natural instinct was to panic and make for the surface once my head went under. I had to calm myself for a few seconds before I continued, slowly abseiling downwards along the rope leading to the seabed ten meters below,

Chaos greeted me on the ocean floor. I joined a human chain of divers kneeling on the seabed, arms linked together to avoid being dragged into the watery abyss by the strong currents. Both dive masters clearly struggled to instruct the other divers what to do next.

Suddenly, a current forced us backwards,

flipping some divers head over heels. After a few terrifying moments, we managed to link arms again. I feared the next strong current would tear someone from our human chain, sending them spiralling into the murky darkness. The dive masters tried to go through some exercises, but it was futile and they finally gave up, giving us the signal to head for the surface.

I had never been so happy to obey an order.

Even though I was anxious to get back on the boat as quickly as possible, Fiona warned us to surface in stages. This was to avoid getting decompression sickness, more commonly known as 'the bends', a potentially deadly build-up of nitrogen bubbles in the blood stream. I found it difficult to maintain my recommended levels but managed to surface without any ill effects.

Back on the boat, I discovered one diver had suffered reverse block in his teeth on the ascent. This happened because a tiny air pocket in one of his dental fillings expanded on the way up, fracturing his tooth. Another person lost a weight-belt while someone else broke a mask. On the journey back, a woman smashed her teeth on a gas tank as the boat hit a wave. With blood pouring from her mouth, she cursed the crew and swore never to dive again. I could understand her anger.

It was such a disappointment. That was not how I imagined my first dive would turn out, with people left angry, sick and bleeding. I began to regret taking the course and wished I had just stayed in St. Lucia and explored the wetlands some more. I went to sleep that night in a despondent mood.

The sea looked slightly calmer the following morning as we headed to sea for another dive. Bad luck continued to dog us as the outboard engine broke down and we had to perform a mid-ocean transfer to another boat. That drama over, I completed the test of diving skills before returning to shore for breakfast. Afterwards, I donned my wetsuit again, this time for a tougher test of skills in rougher sea conditions. Between rough seas and concentrating on carrying out instructions, I didn't have much time to admire my surroundings. By evening, I felt exhausted and wondered would I ever enjoy diving.

We had one more dive to achieve certification and I was dreading the experience. Fortunately, the sea looked much calmer that morning. Once we got to the dive spot, we split into small groups and our dive master Fiona took Mick and myself on our final test of skills. We completed them quickly before going for a pleasure dive.

All the memories of the nightmarish first day disappeared. The fish were out in force after the storm as shafts of lights penetrated the water to illuminate radiant red and yellow coral. Sea plants swayed gently as a brightly painted orange and blue sea slug called a nudibranch crawled slowly along the ocean floor. A clown fish cavorted nearly, mimicking a Spanish flamenco dancer, shimmering in bright red, yellow and blue robes. No ancient coelacanths in sight but I wouldn't have recognised one if it swam up and bit me on the nose.

A curious grouper fish swam to within a foot of my mask, with big, pouting blue lips and tiny black eyes. I nearly laughed aloud inside my mask at the wonder of it all. It was like swimming in an aquarium. If I wanted to investigate something near the seabed, all I had to do was to let some air out of my vest and I slowly dropped down. I floated in an underwater paradise, suspended above the ocean floor, each kick driving me forward, as fish come up to say hello while others scurried away from my path.

There was something hypnotic about the steady inhale and exhale of the air regulator. The suck of my in-breath followed by the burst of bubbles of my out-breath became rhythmic and trance-like. A wonderful sense of calm enveloped me as I floated in this incredible environment. I glanced over at Mick and we exchanged the thumbs-up sign. I felt like an astronaut visiting a strange world. Why would anyone want to travel to Mars when such an alien experience is available a few meters under the waves? I wanted to explore that strange new world forever.

9 SWAZILAND

Even in rural Swaziland, there was no escaping boerewors, the national sausage of South Africa. The Sondzela Backpacker Hostel is situated within the private Mlilwane Wildlife Reserve, but the supper on offer could not rise to its tranquil surroundings. Like the food line of a prison, glum travellers queued outside the kitchen to receive an apologetic plate of boerewors and beans. The al fresco dining more than made up for the food, however I joined others around a large campfire and chewed on rubbery sausages, while watching swarms of flaming cinders take flight into the Swazi sky.

Landlocked by the neighbouring giants of South Africa and Mozambique, Swaziland is approximately the size of Wales, making it one of the smallest countries in Africa. It's also home to the continent's last absolute monarchy, whose king can overrule parliament on any matter. Swaziland gets fewer than 200,000 visitors a year, a fraction of what nearby Kruger National Park enjoys.

Execution Rock

While it lacked many of the animals that Kruger can boast, Mlilwane promised the kind of up-close access to wildlife that its more famous neighbour could only dream of. After checking some maps in the hostel, I opted for a hiking trail leading to the top of the intriguingly named Execution Rock. Rising nearly 4,000 feet above the lovely Ezulwini Valley, or Valley of Heaven in Swazi, it promised to be a demanding hike with great wildlife viewing. I set off the following morning with water and a small packed lunch.

Since there were no lions or other man-eaters in the sanctuary, it was safe to explore the trails without a car or armed ranger.

The first section took me along a gravelled path with little shade. Along the way, I spotted some zebra, impala and a warthog. Some of the animals seemed very tame and didn't run away when approached. After an hour on the trail, I came within sight of the rock itself, an unmistakable peak rising abruptly from the flat surrounding countryside.

I walked towards the hilltop, wasting an hour in a futile search for some bushman cave paintings that were marked on the map, but infuriatingly hard to find. I finally reached the summit and plopped on a boulder to catch my breath, gulping water while taking in the view. The lush greenery of the valley floor spread towards the distant hills. Trees fringed a lake far below that held the promise of more wildlife.

Execution Rock got its name in bygone times when criminals were marched to the summit. They could choose to jump off the cliffs and die with dignity or be encouraged to do so by the tips of prodding spears. The Swazi name of the hill is *Nyonyane*, which means 'little bird'. The word poetically describes with horrifying beauty how these poor souls appeared as they plummeted to their deaths.

I couldn't understand why those ancient authorities went to the bother of forcing those poor wretches to the top of a hill just to kill them. It seemed so pointless.

On the way down, I passed the small lake I had viewed from the summit, called Hippo Pool. True to its name, a number of hippos sunbathed on a small, grassy island in the middle of the pond. Nearby, I was surprised to spot a crocodile lounging on the banks, its jaws agape. I hadn't realised there were crocodiles in the sanctuary.

Ted Reilly

Back at the hostel, I took a refreshing dip in the nearby natural spring pool. To my horror that evening, boerewors were on the menu yet again, but I was too hungry to care. I brought my supper out to the garden and asked a man reading a book if I could share his table. I guessed he was in his mid-sixties and we soon fell into a conversation about my walk that day. He introduced himself as Ted Reilly.

"Not *the* Ted Reilly?" I asked. He nodded. The man seated before me was a living legend in Swaziland and responsible for almost single-handedly bringing the country's wildlife back from the dead. I pushed my plate of sausages aside and asked him to tell me how he first got into wildlife conservation. He joined his hands together, as if about to pray.

"Did you know that in the early 1900s, wildlife in Swaziland was so plentiful it was termed 'vermin'?" he asked, raising his eyebrows. "Hunters even used machine guns and poisoned water holes. Nobody thought it was possible to wipe out game animals in Swaziland," he said, shaking his head ruefully. "They were wrong."

He spoke slowly and carefully, closing his eyes at times as if the memories he summoned were painful. "My father owned a farm and mined tin. When I took over the family business, wildlife in

144

Swaziland had nearly been exterminated by hunting. I couldn't just stand by and do nothing so I offered the farm to the King of Swaziland for wildlife protection and it became the country's first protected sanctuary in 1964. After a century-long absence, rhino were one of the first species reintroduced. Giraffe followed soon after."

His success drew admirers and visitors, but also poachers, especially for rhino and their valuable horns. Rhino horn is made of keratin, exactly the same type of protein that forms our hair and fingernails. Even though it has been scientifically proven as effective as chewing your own nails, powdered rhino horn fetches around $60,000 a kilo for use in traditional Chinese medicine.

With that kind of money involved, poaching became big business and attracted highly organised criminals. The death of a rhino usually resulted from a telephone call from Hong Kong. High tech criminals in helicopters locate and immobilise the animal from the air. The GPS coordinates of the rhino are sent to heavily armed poachers on the ground, who then remove the horn, leaving the butchered animal to bleed to death.

"Was poaching a big problem for you at the beginning?" I asked.

"It sure was and always has been," he said, rubbing his tired eyes. "At the start, the poachers were armed with machine guns and our rangers only had clubs and spears. During the so-called Rhino Wars, we were losing an animal every two weeks and it had to stop. We armed our rangers with automatic weapons and that helped level the playing field a bit. But it was the Game Act that turned the tide in our favour."

The Game Act of 1991 is a highly effective piece of conservation legislation, initiated and drafted by Ted Reilly. If caught, a poacher faced between five and fifteen years imprisonment. The act also gave rangers unprecedented powers of search and arrest, anywhere in the country. They could carry arms and, controversially, are immune from prosecution if they killed anyone in the course of their duty.

"Since the Game Act came into force, only three rhinos have been lost to poaching," he said, jabbing his finger on the table. "It's a tough law but it aims to prevent poaching, not put people in jail."

Ted glanced at his watch. "Sorry, but I must be going," he said, rising slowly from the wooden bench. "They'll be expecting me back at the lodge." I stood up to shake his hand and wished him all the best with his future work. Thanks to him, Swaziland now has a number of well-run wildlife parks for the enjoyment of locals and visitors alike. When people talk about wildlife conservation in Africa, the name Ted Reilly should never be far away.

The King, Gaddafi and I

Along with Dan and Jason, a couple of backpackers I befriended at the hostel, I caught a bus to the local market the following morning. Having picked up a few words of Swazi from the hostel staff, I felt I was ready to put them into action.

"Sawbono," I greeted a stall-owner.

"Sawbono, unjani," he replied with a bright smile.

"Yebo," I replied.

The exchange was little more than the usual 'Hi, how're you? I'm fine, you? Fine, thanks' small talk we hear every day. I repeated this exchange many times during my short stay in Swaziland and each time, the interaction felt genuine and unforced. The people treated me as a person, not as if I had a dollar sign hanging over my head. It was such a relief after South Africa. I walked happily amongst the people, feeling light and carefree.

After browsing several stalls, I bought a few souvenirs, including a huge flag of Swaziland. No idea what I planned to use it for, but it looked great with its black and white cowhide shield imposed over two spears.

I found Dan taking photographs of some of the vendors and their wares. Dan was inseparable from his professional-grade camera and rightly proud of the fantastic photos he took.

"Got some good shots of the stall owners," he said, carefully placing the camera in his bag. We found Jason sitting at a nearby food stall, drinking coffee and watching the world go by.

"Ready to move on?" I asked him.

"Sure, whatever," he replied, tossing the dregs of his coffee onto the dusty ground before joining us.

Walking along the main street, I noticed a simple mural painted on a wall. It depicted a set of parents weeping before the open coffin of their son, surrounded by sad onlookers. The message daubed above it read 'AIDS KILLS — SAY NO TO SEX.' The disease is a huge problem in Africa, but it seems to have hit little Swaziland worse than most. An estimated 35% of the Swazi population have AIDS, one of the highest rates in the world. This rate of infection is crippling for such a small country.

In an attempt to mitigate the AIDS pandemic in 2001, the king used his traditional powers to invoke a time-honoured chastity rite, which encouraged all Swazi maidens to abstain from sexual relations for five years. However, only two months after imposing the ban, he violated his own decree when he chose a sixteen-year-old girl to be his 13th wife. For breaking the decree, he was fined a cow, which he duly paid.

As we ambled along, Dan stopped dead in his

tracks, staring at a nearby wall. I followed his gaze to a poster, which declared, 'Gaddafi to meet the king today!'

"Not *the* Gaddafi," Jason wondered aloud. Subsequent inquiries confirmed that the king of Swaziland planned to meet Colonel Gaddafi of Libya at a nearby sports stadium that day. Apparently, the Libyan leader was on a tour of sub-Saharan states. This was an opportunity we couldn't miss, so we caught a taxi to Lobamba to see the action.

The King and his guest were not due to arrive for another hour so we purchased some snacks and sat on an earthen embankment outside the stadium. A procession of women passed by, each of them wrapped in a colourful, full-body shawl and each carrying a tall reed, swaying above their heads. Once we finished our snacks, we followed the crowd inside. The stadium was a simple affair, having only one small covered stand but with lovely views of the distant mountains. The women gathered in the middle of the field, holding up a small sea of reeds that swayed gently in the breeze. Police and photographers milled around, awaiting the arrival of the king and his infamous guest.

Women carrying reeds to meet the Swazi king

"Says here the current king of Swaziland has fifteen wives," Dan said, reading from his guidebook.

"Where does he get the energy?" Jason asked, barely able to hide his amazement.

"That's nothing," scoffed Dan. "Apparently, his father had over 120 wives."

I craned my neck toward the entrance each time there was a bit of excitement, hoping to catch a glimpse of the man dubbed by Ronald Reagan as the 'mad dog of the Middle-East.' It was Gaddafi I wanted to see. The man was a tyrant and accused of sponsoring terrorism around the world but here we were, excitedly waiting his arrival as if he were a pop star.

People jostled and pushed to get a better view. I forced my way onto a wooden stand, opposite the main viewing platform. After a long and tiring wait, there was a rush of excitement, as black cars with tinted windows pulled up outside the stadium. The first to enter was the Queen Mother, followed by her entourage. She wore a white headband, which held a single, red feather. She also carried a traditional knobkerrie stick, which is like a walking stick with a thick knob at the end.

A buzz went up from the crowd when King Mswati III entered the stadium alongside the unmistakable figure of Gaddafi. The Libyan dictator wore his signature dark sunglasses while the king wore a crown of three orange feathers on the back of his head. Gaddafi saluted the cheering crowd, smiling broadly and giving the thumbs-up sign as he passed. He came within a few feet of me and, for a split second, seemed to look right at me. His hard-faced security men glared at me with hate and distain. By then, the leaders had passed and taken their seats on the main viewing platform.

This was like a dream for Dan, who fired off photos of each dignitary in quick succession. Once Gaddafi was seated, Dan broke from the crowd and daringly stood feet from the dictator, taking photo after photo. Gaddafi's security guards looked at each other anxiously, unsure about how to respond to such an act of boldness. Dan returned with a huge smile, happily accepting the high-fives that came his way.

Gaddafi of Libya with the King of Swaziland

A smartly-suited man tried to push his way onto my spot, but I held my ground, refusing to yield an inch. He looked at me with bewilderment.

"Do you please mind? This is my place," he insisted.

"Sorry, but who do you think you are?" I retorted, squaring up to him.

"I am the minister for foreign affairs so please move NOW."

"Well, why didn't you say so," I thought, as I

meekly surrendered my place to the government minister and joined the crowd below the stand. Gaddafi was treated to a show of traditional Swazi dancing. For me, the show was over and we left the stadium shortly after.

It was a pity I only had a few days in such an interesting and welcoming country as Swaziland. I'd only scratched the surface of the tiny kingdom and there was so much more to see. Mlilwane gave me a taste for wildlife but I wanted more. The main course lay just to the north and that was where I was heading next.

9 KRUGER

If there was one place in South Africa that excited me more than any other, it was Kruger National Park. The world-famous wildlife reserve is synonymous with the country and taking a Kruger safari is almost compulsory for any foreign visitor. Along with Dan and Jason, I inquired about safaris at Sondzela in Swaziland. We were presented with a long list of safari packages, from a bare-bones do-it-yourself experience to private reserves where animals personally wake you up in the morning. We opted for one of the cheaper packages, costing 1,200 rand including food and all park fees.

The next day, we caught the Baz Bus from Swaziland to Nelspruit, where we overnighted before getting a connecting bus to Kruger. The six-hour drive from Nelspruit to Kruger Park brought us through the little-explored province of Mpumalanga. Power plants and endless cornfields dominated the passing landscape. This was part of the *lowveld*, the flat low-lying eastern part of the country. Soon, we climbed sharply towards the *highveld* and the dramatic Drakensburg Escarpment. This sudden change in altitude gives South Africa some of its most spectacular scenery.

Along the route, we passed through the old mining town of Pilgrim's Rest. Gold was discovered nearby in 1873, sparking a gold rush and instantly creating settlements such as Pilgrim's Rest. The town boasted quaint, Victorian-style buildings along with busloads of tourists. Jason wasn't impressed.

"We've got bucket loads of old mining towns like these in Australia," he said with a yawn.

Later, we stopped at a scenic viewpoint called God's Window. With a name like that, it had to be good. Unfortunately, a thick blanket of fog meant that God had the curtains firmed drawn that day. I stared out into the greyness, futilely trying to imagine what the view must be like.

We didn't delay and drove on towards our next stop, Burke's Luck Potholes. This is a collection of strange rock formations formed by the swirling waters of the Blyde River. Apparently, Burke was a gold prospector who spent two fruitless years in the area before giving up, only for the next prospector to hit it lucky.

By the time we reached Blyde River Canyon, the

fog had lifted. I walked from the minibus to the edge of the world's third largest canyon and joined others in letting my jaw hit the ground. The 20-mile-long canyon was so vast, I had trouble comprehending it was real. The canyon floor seemed miles deep, punctuated by three rounded hills known as the Three Rondavels. There was very little chatter as people appreciated what must be one of nature's most amazing sights. In the face of such vast beauty, I felt small and insignificant. A ledge peeked over the precipice and I asked someone to take a photo before nervously inching out onto the ledge. Staring into the vastness with my feet dangling hundreds of feet above the canyon floor, I felt I was on the very edge of the world.

It was almost dark when we finally entered Kruger National Park at the Orpen Gate. A short time later, we arrived at the Tamboti Rest Camp, my home while on safari. A high wire fence surrounded the camp, a necessary measure considering what roamed outside. My quarters consisted of a khaki-coloured safari tent, with mattress and blanket. It was roomy and ideal for my needs. I shared a few beers with Dan and Jason before heading to bed. We had an early rise ahead of us.

Hanging out at Blyde River Canyon

As I lay in my tent, I tried to imagine what my first safari would be like. I pictured myself (wearing a pith helmet) in the back of an open jeep, protected by an armed ranger who kept an eye out for elephant dung and leopard tracks. After seeing lions, leopards and rhino around a water hole, I'd retire back to the camp to regale fellow travellers of the incredible sights I'd seen.

The following morning, however, I sleepily climbed aboard a large, comfortable minibus. I noticed that many passengers carried binoculars and I cursed myself for forgetting to bring such an important piece of wildlife-spotting equipment.

"My name is Malcolm and I will be your safari guide," said the large man in the front passenger seat. He held a walkie-talkie as he spoke. "I will try to make sure we see as many animals as possible but please understand, these are wild animals and they sometimes make it hard for us to find them. Okay, so let's go."

Calling an area the size of Wales a park is a bit misleading. There are no nicely divided areas for zebras, lions and giraffes. This is the wild and animals are free to roam and kill where they want. The park has a well-developed road system and plenty of accommodation for the 1.5 million visitors each year. Forming a long wedge along the border with Zimbabwe and Mozambique, the park is bounded to the north by the Limpopo River and south by the Crocodile River. The dry, summer months are the best time to visit, as the chance of malaria is lower and vegetation is sparse, allowing you a better chance to view elusive wildlife.

The Big Five used to be the prized trophies of colonial hunters, but are now the most coveted sightings of the Kruger. Rhino, elephant, lion, buffalo and leopard are even featured on South African currency. We first encountered a herd of giraffe grazing on the topmost leaves of a tree, causing everyone to reach for their cameras and begin snapping furiously. A German couple produced a notebook with each animal listed and ticked off a box next to the giraffe. Dan leaned out the passenger window with his camouflaged, super-long zoom lens, ready to photograph the first thing that moved. That was the type of hunting we could all enjoy.

On both sides of the road, dozens of ever-watchful Impala took fright as we approached, sending them bounding into the bush in unison. They reminded me of a shoal of fish, darting and changing direction with impressive synchronisation. They are the most plentiful animal in the park with a population of around 100,000. Impala are literally the fast food of Kruger. With their doe-like eyes and large numbers, they are ideal prey for predators, which is pretty much every other animal.

After lunch, we drove off the main road towards a water hole where a herd of wallowing buffalos. To me, they looked like a dour-faced herd of black cattle, adorned with immense curled horns.

"Cape Buffalos are dangerous despite looking docile. They are much feared," Malcolm said. "Buffalo are very unpredictable and can be hard to kill because of those thick horns. Not even lions would tackle a herd of buffalo."

The radio crackled into life and Malcolm spoke into it before telling the driver to reverse and get back onto the road.

"Lions have been spotted up ahead," he said. An excited buzz travelled around the van, as we peered out the window, straining to see them. We needn't have worried, as a long queue of vehicles signalled their location. We joined the queue and waited for our turn. Eventually, we pulled up alongside two lions lounging by the roadside, a male and female. Dan extended his camera lens out the passenger window and shot frame after frame, barely concealing his glee.

"The female lions do most of the work in a lion pride, hunting and caring for the young," our guide whispered. "The males don't do very much except rest and can sleep up to 20 hours a day."

The last comment provoked a Dutch woman seated behind me to remark on the similarity with her husband, much to the delight of the other female passengers.

"The male lion is also capable of incredible bouts of sexual activity during the mating season," smiled Malcolm, "up to fifty times a day."

I whooped and high-fived Jason at that information, much to the disgruntlement of the Dutch lady.

Even from behind the slightly open window of the van, I was afraid to lean out too far. Both lions took no notice of us as they rested by the roadside. The male was a huge creature, the size of a small pony. A regal mane of shaggy, reddish hair framed his cold, calculating face. He stared at me with his powerful, orange-tinted eyes. I could almost imagine him thinking, "That's right pal, just lean out a little more and I can tear your head off before you can pull yourself back inside."

The lions were surrounded by tourist-filled vans but they didn't budge. Any other animal would have bolted long before, but not lions. This was their turf, their kingdom and they were going to move when they were ready and not a second earlier. They saw we were no threat, merely a passing inconvenience. How many times can a human being be made feel so insignificant by an animal?

Seriously impressive creatures, these lions.

I asked Malcolm about lion attacks after we departed. He exhaled deeply before answering.

"Yes, we've had unfortunate incidents where tourists have been killed by lions. They seem to forget this is a wild place and these are wild animals. They forget this is not a zoo. One family from Korea spotted some elephants last year and left their car to pose for photographs. They never realised the danger and were stampeded to death," he admitted sadly.

"What do you do if you meet a lion in the bush?" asked Jason.

"If you come upon a lion on foot, you have a chance of scaring it away if you stand your ground and don't run. No chance if it's a leopard though, they'll attack you no matter what you do."

"Some chance of that," whispered Jason. "I can't see myself standing still if I ever meet a lion. I'd probably just piss my pants and run as fast as I bloody could."

Nothing compares to seeing animals in the wild, in their natural habitat, doing what animals do when people encounter them — mainly, running away. Comparing this to the experience of a zoo, I always felt sorry watching a caged lion pacing up and down along its enclosure, while fat tourists snapped pictures just beyond the reach of its deadly claws. It must have been a form of torture for the poor animal, helplessly watching easy meals amble a few feet away. Not a great way for the king of the jungle to live.

After returning to the rest camp that evening, I discovered why the safari was so cheap. Malcolm called me over before handing me a sharp kitchen knife.

"Everyone has to pitch in with the cooking. It's Spaghetti Bolognese tonight," Malcolm declared. I helped chop dozens of peppers, while Dan and Jason boiled spaghetti in a vast cauldron.

As we gorged on pasta around the campfire, Malcolm told us that over the past five years, 12,000 immigrants from neighbouring Mozambique had been arrested trying to cross illegally into South Africa at Kruger.

"One family was crossing when they

encountered a pride of lions and fled up a tree for safely," Malcolm said, helping himself to more spaghetti. "The lions waited and picked them off one at a time. Once they realised how easy they were to kill, they just waited for them to fall asleep and fall out of the tree."

Malcolm paused and stared into the inky darkness beyond the wire fence.

"When rangers came upon them, only one boy was left alive. The rangers chased and killed the lions. It had to be done. Once a lion realises how easy humans are to kill, they are sure to attack again." Malcolm stopped eating and took a deep breath. "I can't imagine the horror of what that poor boy went through, watching his family die one by one, and waiting for his turn to come. Nobody knows exactly how many immigrants are killed by lions, but we find shoes or bloody clothing in the bush pretty often."

"Hey, look over there," shouted Jason. Malcolm shone his torch towards the fence where his beam picked out a pair of hideous red eyes glowing in the darkness. A spotted hyena was snooping for food along the fence, prowling back and forth with its head low to the ground. Dan broke off a piece of bread and approached the fence. "I wouldn't do that," warned Malcolm. "Those guys have very powerful jaws and could easily rip your arm off if you get too close."

Dan thought better of it and retreated back to his seat. Later, an elephant came up to then fence, but again, Malcolm asked us not to feed it as it might become dependent on the camp for food.

"An elephant consumes up to 200 kilos of vegetation a day," Malcolm told me, as I took a few photographs of our evening visitor. "A herd can have a potentially destructive effect on the environment and this has to be controlled by culling or translocation."

"Is it true they have their own funerals?" asked Dan, causing Jason to burst out laughing at the idea.

"It's true. They are sensitive animals and mourn the deaths of relatives by elaborate funeral ceremonies. They also have huge gatherings which seem to be meetings of some kind."

Just as Malcolm sought volunteers for the washing up, I slinked off to climb onto the nearby water tower and admire the jungle canopy. Roars and screams of unknown creatures echoed throughout the terrifying world beyond the fence. At that moment, there was probably another desperate family from Mozambique preparing to cross illegally into the country. I imagined them packing their paltry possessions before setting out on foot across this wilderness in the darkness of night. The thought filled me with terror.

The president of the Transvaal, Paul Kruger,

created the park in 1898 to protect animals from European hunters who threatened them with extinction. Today, over 1.5 million people visit the park every year. In 1975, the apartheid government erected a high-security fence along the northern Mozambique border.

A war of independence raged in Mozambique and the apartheid government in South Africa feared some form of cross-border contamination from these freedom-minded troublemakers. This had the effect of cutting off the traditional migration route of elephants from Kruger to Mozambique. Those on the warring side were slaughtered for their meat and valuable ivory. The fence was dismantled after the end of apartheid. In 2002, an agreement was signed creating a giant cross-border park, encompassing Kruger, Gonarezhou of Zimbabwe and Limpopo of Mozambique. It formed the Great Limpopo Transfrontier Park, a wildlife reserve roughly the size of Belgium.

The next day was overcast and a steady drizzle accompanied us during our safari. The viewing was disappointing, as we only saw a jackal and a dead impala in a tree.

"The weather is not good today," Malcolm apologised, pointing to the grey rainclouds. "The animals are hiding and don't want to get wet any more than we do."

Malcolm's eyesight was incredible. He could spot birds hiding in thick foliage where I only saw leaves. By the end of the day, the sight of a herd of giraffe loping through the open savannah elicited a yawn and a sarcastic, "boring" from a wag at the back.

On the way back to camp, we stopped to watch a dozen elephants crossing the road, trunk to tail. It was an amazing sight.

"Elephants are very social and live in families led by the mother," Malcolm told us. "The female matriarch is the leader and the herd follow her everywhere. Elephants are also very intelligent and are one of the few animals that can recognise themselves in a mirror. As I mentioned to some of you last night, they also show grief around the bones of dead relatives."

I absolutely loved these little bits of obscure knowledge that Malcolm dispensed.

A park ranger sped past us trying to head off some tourists who had left their car and were approaching the elephants to get better photographs.

"Fastest way to get killed in Kruger," Malcolm said, shaking his head.

That evening at the camp, Malcolm told us about the impressive defences of the arcadia tree. When animals munch the tree, the damaged leaves release a chemical into the air, which alerts the remaining leaves of imminent danger. These leaves quickly produce a foul-tasting substance, which soon makes the leaves unpalatable. The animal then moves away, giving the tree time to recover.

The Big Five is only the tip of the animal iceberg in Kruger. The park teems with birds of incredible colours, various species of crawlers, diggers and burrowers, each with their own unique characteristics. As we got ready to leave Kruger the next morning, we took turns to thank Malcolm and give him a richly deserved tip. When I shook his hand, I asked him would he ever consider doing any other job.

"Not a chance," he smiled as he pocketed my tip. After everything I'd experienced over the last three days, I found it impossible to disagree with him.

10 JOHANNESBURG

"All roads lead to Johannesburg" — *Alan Paton: Cry,*
The Beloved Country

I thought the hostel owner was kidding when he
suggested I share a room with his two Rottweilers.
The Baz Bus had deposited me at Pretoria's
Hatfield Backpackers Hostel late that evening. To
my dismay, the manager informed me the hostel
was fully booked. The Baz Bus had departed by
then and I was in no mood to go roaming the dark
streets of the former Transvaal capital in search of
accommodation. I pleaded with the owner if he had
anything at all left. He showed me the small room
where his two slavering Rottweilers slept. When he
opened the door, both dogs cocked their heads and
let out a blood-curdling bark that made me take a

169

few steps backwards.

"Don't worry about them," the owner assured me, "they're more likely to lick you to death than rip you to pieces." With a wicked smile, he wished me goodnight and closed the door. I lay on the bed, daring not move a muscle as my ears strained to each moan from the deadly dogs slumbering at my bedside. Even the nights spent amongst the wild animals in Kruger didn't frighten me as much. Every time one of them groaned, I thought it would be the last sound I'd hear before they leapt onto my bed and tore my throat open.

I didn't sleep well that night.

Grumpy and unrested, I visited the Voortrekker Monument the following morning. Perched on a small hill just outside Pretoria city centre, the monument resembled a grey, expressionless, stone cube. It was built between 1938 and 1949 to commemorate the Great Trek, a series of migrations that established the old Boer republics of the Orange Free State and Transvaal. *Boer* is the Dutch word for farmer and describes the descendants of early Dutch settlers in South Africa, later known as Afrikaners. A statue of a Trek leader stood guard on each corner of the great stone building. A wall, carved with wagons in the defensive *laager* formation, surrounded the monument. Inside, the main attraction was a series of marble panels telling the story of the Voortrekkers, the Boers who took part in the Great

Trek.

When British rule became too much for the original Boer settlers of the Cape, they decided to leave and head into the wild hinterland of Africa in search of a place where they could carry on their way of life in peace. Between 1835 and 1854, the Boers embarked on a number of such migrations or *treks*.

The first series of panels depict the Boers leaving their settlements on the Cape in 1835, a scene reminiscent of a Wild West movie. Bearded men on horseback armed with rifles rode alongside wagons loaded with family possessions. Behind the men, bonnet-clad women herded sheep and cattle.

Piet Retief led one band of trekkers across the Drakensberg Mountains into Zululand. He negotiated with the Zulu Chief, Dingane, who agreed to give them land to live on. A panel shows Retief signing the treaty with Dingane. A young servant is seated on the ground beside Dingane, his hands cupped to act as a spittoon. Dingane feared that if his spit hit the ground, witchdoctors might use it in magic against him. After the treaty was signed, Dingane changed his mind and became fearful of the Voortrekkers. He had Retief and his party taken to a nearby hill where they were clubbed to death. Retief was last to die, forced to watch his comrades and son murdered in a horrible manner.

The subsequent panels show the Zulu army attacking Boer settlements. A woman tries to shield her child as a Zulu warrior stands over her with his spear. No doubt, these were scenes designed to make Boer blood boil.

After these setbacks, the Voortrekkers were in disarray and morale was low. Many of the trek leaders were dead and some had already returned to the Cape. Enter Andres Pretorius, a wealthy farmer who agreed to become their new leader. He quickly organised a *commando*, a mobile unit of 500 fighting men, and led them into a decisive engagement to avenge those killed. The Zulu army that opposed them, however, was nearly 12,000 strong and the chances of a Boer victory seemed remote. It was then the Voortrekkers made a vow that if God gave them victory, they would commemorate the day forever.

On December 16, 1838, a date that became known as the Day of the Vow, the Voortrekkers defeated the Zulu army on the banks of Blood River. An estimated 3,000 Zulus died, while the Voortrekkers sustained only minor losses. For the victors, it confirmed that God was on their side and blessed their mission to conquer the native tribes. With the creation of the Transvaal Republic and Orange Free State, the Boers finally found a place where they could rest. On December 16 every year, a shaft of sunlight falls directly on a plaque inside the monument bearing the inscription 'ONS VIR

JOU SUID-AFRIKA' or 'We for thee, South Africa.'

Once I returned to the hostel, I couldn't bear the thought of another night with my two canine companions, so I checked out and booked into North-South. I found it much nicer and had the added advantage of being able to share a room with humans instead of dogs.

I walked into town the following day and explored Church Square, which despite warnings to the contrary, seemed safe enough. A large statue of Paul Kruger, former president of the Transvaal Republic, dominated the square. Old colonial buildings encircled office workers enjoying lunch on nearby park benches.

I visited Kruger's former residence just off the main street. It was a sparse place with little of immediate interest. However, it was there a touching scene played out over a century prior. In June of 1900, Transvaal was close to defeat in the Boer War and British troops approached Pretoria. President Kruger was preparing to leave the city before their arrival. His wife was too ill to travel and insisted on remaining behind. They knew no harm would come to her and she would be well treated by the courteous British. Kruger had little time to say his goodbyes, spending a few precious minutes alone with his wife before departing. He would never see her again.

On the way back to the hostel, I stopped at a

small diner and discovered the Afrikaner pastry called *vetkoek*, a pocket of deep-fried dough, filled with minced meat and gravy. It was both tasty and cheap, an ideal backpacker meal. Back at North-South, I chatted to the owner John, a fellow Irishman from County Down.

"I came here a long time ago and joined the police force. I loved my time with them. After that, I joined the South African Armed Forces and took part in some pretty hairy missions in Angola," he laughed.

I asked him how he felt about the new government.

"How can you have democracy when most of the blacks are so backward?" he asked. He started flicking the light-switch on and off. "When I first hired blacks to work here, they thought this was some kind of magic. To them, we're like astronauts with our technology. How can you give such backward people a say in the running of a modern country?" He continued flicking the light on and off.

I had enough. I tried not to be judgmental about the racist attitudes of some people I met but I couldn't take this any longer.

"Stop," I pleaded, standing up. "This has to stop. I've had enough of this racist shit. What's your problem with black people, what have they done to you?"

"What do you know?" he retorted, "You mean well but you haven't been here long enough. After you've been here as long as I have, then see if you have the same opinions."

"Maybe," I replied, "but I know racism is just wrong."

I left the room, the light still flicking on and off. I left the hostel the following day and moved to another down the road.

Pretoria was relatively safe compared to the war zone that was Johannesburg. According to many people I spoke to, crime was out of control and my guidebook warned against visiting the city centre. Private armies posing as neighbourhood security provided protection for those who could afford it. This was the city that created the *blaster*, the world's first flame-throwing car. It was designed in response to a sharp rise in carjackings while motorists stopped at red lights. Now, all a driver had to do was press a button and flames would shoot from under the car, possibly incinerating the would-be attacker. This wasn't a scene from Mad Max or some other post-apocalyptic film.

No, this was Johannesburg.

Soweto

After the end of the Great Trek, the Boer republic of Transvaal was a simple place, dominated by farmers and churchgoers. That was until gold was discovered near modern-day Johannesburg in 1884, changing everything. Miners and powerful capitalists such as Cecil Rhodes flocked to the area. By 1896, the city of Johannesburg came into being with a population of 100,000, one of the fastest city growths of all time.

Mining jobs led to an influx of black workers from the surrounding countryside. They were forced into settlements on the city outskirts so authorities could control their movements while keeping them close enough to be used as cheap labour. These settlements became known as Soweto, an acronym for Southwestern Townships.

Soweto encompasses 33 different townships with a combined population of over 1.2 million people, spanning an area of 70 square miles. A visit to this infamous area during the apartheid days used to be foolhardy, but tours have now operated safely for years. A tour bus picked me up from my accommodation the following day. Joshua Jankie runs daily tours to Soweto and promises to give the visitor 'the good, the bad and the ugly' of the city.

Joshua's tour first stopped at the Hector Pieterson Memorial and Museum, named after the first student killed during the Soweto Uprising in

1976. On June 16 that year, black students organised a peaceful protest against the introduction of Afrikaans as the language of instruction to their schools. The students marched up Vilakazi Street where police confronted them. When the demonstrators refused to disperse, the police fired tear gas into the crowd and, soon after, started shooting. Thirteen-year-old Hector Pieterson was the first to be shot dead but, by the end of the day, over a hundred of his fellow students were also killed. As we drove along Vilakazi Street, I tried to imagine the scenes of chaos that day. Today, the area is part of the upscale East Orlando, where Nelson Mandela and Archbishop Desmond Tutu once lived. According to Joshua, it was the only street in the world to have housed two Nobel Peace Prize winners.

The tour proceeded to the Deepcliff area where the emerging middle-class and thousands of slum-dwellers live side by side. These shacks housed large families of six or more and were made of corrugated iron, wood and cardboard. Conditions were appalling but, despite that, visitors are greeted with smiles. Given the recent history of white oppression, this open friendliness was almost embarrassing.

"One of the ways the apartheid system classified people was by using the pencil test," Joshua told us. "Sometimes, there was a doubt if a person should be classified as white or coloured. To solve this, they stuck a pencil in your hair and, if it stuck, you were classified as coloured. If it didn't, you were classified as white."

"Do you know the story of Sandra Laing?" asked one of the passengers.

"Ah yes," replied Joshua, "She was the slightly dark-skinned daughter of two white parents but was subjected to the pencil test and classified as coloured. She was expelled from her all-white school and her family shunned."

I shook my head in disbelief. If anything demonstrated the total absurdity of the apartheid system, it was this. A pencil decided the kind of education you received, where you lived and whom you married. It would be laughable if it hadn't adversely affected so many lives.

"Illegal immigration from other countries is also a problem," admitted Joshua. "Housing projects are slowing down because of this and it can lead to tension and violence between locals and immigrants."

However, there is hope. Self-employment is rising and one in five of those employed now actually work in Soweto. The area is no longer a mere labour store for white factories in Johannesburg. The government is building thousands of new houses for the slum-dwellers, while medical clinics and health advice are freely available.

"Progress is slow, but the people now have the freedom to achieve a better life", beamed Joshua. "The people don't want hand-outs. They are willing to be patient and wait a little longer for the rewards."

My time in South Africa was coming to an end. As one adventure ended, another would begin with my journey to Australia. As I packed my bags for the last time in South Africa, I tried to sum up my time in the country.

I fondly remembered looking out over Cape Town from the summit of Table Mountain, diving with Great White sharks, learning about Xhosa, Zulu and Afrikaner cultures, meeting the people of Swaziland, and seeing the incredible wildlife of Kruger. I fondly recalled the friendly people, the stunning scenery, glorious beaches and great beer.

So much had been left unseen. I hadn't visited the Boer War battlefields, where so many died and so many heroes were made. I hadn't seen the interior, the old Orange Free State and Bloemfontein, where the British started concentration camps after the war. I hadn't hiked the Drakensburg Mountains. There was so much left to see, a return visit seemed certain.

I decided the one thing I would remember most, however, was the low-grade sense of fear everywhere I went, like a mild headache that disrupted each day. Whites lived in fear of blacks and blacks lived in fear of gangsters and the police. I was constantly warned, 'Don't go there', 'be sure to take a taxi', 'this area is safe' or 'that area is not safe'. Rich people lived behind walls topped with razor wire and drove bulletproof cars.

Was this the Rainbow Nation that Archbishop Desmond Tutu spoke of? Racism was still alive and the gulf between rich and poor may even have increased. Crime was out of control in some cities and educated whites, badly needed in South Africa, had fled overseas. The faces of government had changed but many of the same problems remained.

With my backpack bulging with freshly laundered clothes, I checked my tickets to Australia and made sure I had my passport. I sat on the dorm bed one last time, holding *Long Walk to Freedom* in my hands. I looked at Mandela's face on the cover and smiled. He had informed me, educated me and sometimes confused me on my way through South Africa. When I encountered people with hateful views, I silently recited his words 'If they can be taught to hate, they can be taught to love.' His was the story of a modern saint, not a politician. I had carried him across his land and listened to his whispered wisdom. His book had been such a part of my journey through South Africa, I considered mailing it back to Ireland. But that is not what Mandela would have done. With great effort, I heaved the backpack onto my shoulders and left the dorm. Before leaving the hostel, I placed the Great Book on a table in the communal room for the next traveller to pick up and read.

Mandela's long walk was done. Mine was only beginning.

FROM THE AUTHOR

Thank you for reading *Cape Town to Kruger*, I sincerely hope you enjoyed it. I'd love to hear from you so please stop by **JohnDwyerBooks.com** where you can:

- Contact me via Facebook, Twitter or email
- Check out my other books
- Browse my travel photos and videos from around the world
- Read my travel articles and blog posts
- Subscribe to my newsletter and be the **FIRST** to know when I have a new book out

OTHER BOOKS BY JOHN DWYER

Praise for **High Road to Tibet: Travels in China, Tibet, Nepal and India**

'John Dwyer might be just the ticket to fill [Michael] Palin's well-worn shoes.' — HungryFeet.com

'You [John Dwyer] really do give an authentic feeling of the contrasting atmospheres as you move from place to place.' — Dervla Murphy, international best-selling travel author

Praise for **Klondike House: Memories of an Irish Country Childhood**

'As you read this book, you will be in the company of someone whose childhood was interwoven into the fabric of West Cork and who still loves the soul of his own place.' — Alice Taylor, international best-selling author of '*To School Through The Fields*'

'The author has a wonderful ability to engage the reader and draw them into the past alongside him...The ways of Ireland's past are sadly disappearing, but as long as people like John are around, they will remain a part of who we are today.' — John Dolan, Cork Evening Echo

Made in the USA
Charleston, SC
23 May 2015